Studies in the Modern Russian Language

GENERAL EDITOR: DENNIS WARD

Professor of Russian, University of Edinburgh

7

ELEMENT ORDER

R. BIVON

Lecturer in Russian,
University of East Anglia

CAMBRIDGE
AT THE UNIVERSITY PRESS
1971

CAMBRIDGE UNIVERSITY PRESS
Cambridge, New York, Melbourne, Madrid, Cape Town, Singapore, São Paulo, Delhi

Cambridge University Press
The Edinburgh Building, Cambridge CB2 8RU, UK

Published in the United States of America by Cambridge University Press, New York

www.cambridge.org
Information on this title: www.cambridge.org/9780521110792

First published 1971
This digitally printed version 2009

A catalogue record for this publication is available from the British Library

Library of Congress Catalogue Card Number: 76–134612

ISBN 978-0-521-08025-5 hardback
ISBN 978-0-521-11079-2 paperback

CONTENTS

NOTE

Throughout this work, the source Известия Академии Наук СССР, серия литературы и языка, is abbreviated to Изв АН СССР, сер лит и яз.

INTRODUCTION

Word order in Russian is said to be freer than in English and this freedom may be exploited to 'express varied shades of meaning and emphasis' (Borras and Christian, p. 376). Borras and Christian add that 'this freedom of word order is part of the idiomatic structure of the language'. Freedom of word order in Russian has often misleadingly been confused with arbitrariness. This study sets out to examine the factors underlying this so-called 'free' word order in Russian and to apply them to a number of commonly occurring grammatical structures in order to elucidate which 'shades of meaning and emphasis' are involved.

The present work is restricted in its scope to the written 'literary language' (литературный язык). Certain of the functions of word order in the written language are taken over by intonation in the spoken language. Intonation plays no part in determining word order in the written language except where this is attempting to imitate the spoken language as, for example, in plays, in dialogue in works of prose or in language written in a colloquial style.

The subject of this study has so far been called 'word order'. In fact, the subject which is commonly called 'word order' is much wider in scope than this: it is not only concerned with the order of individual words but also with that of various groupings of words. These various groupings of words, as well as individual words, will be defined below (see part I, section 2) and called 'elements of structure' or simply 'elements'. Therefore, the subject treated in this work will be referred to broadly as 'element order', the term 'word order' being restricted to the order of individual words within a group (see part I, section 2). Part II will be concerned with the order of three grammatical elements—clauses and groups as well as words themselves.

As there is no satisfactory generally accepted grammatical analysis of Russian, it has been found necessary to describe the methods of grammatical analysis employed in this work. This is indispensable to the full understanding of part II. This grammatical analysis is not intended to be at all exhaustive but is an attempt to explain the grammatical terms which will be used in part II. Previous works on 'word order' have either used the ill-defined terminology of traditional Soviet grammar (Sirotinina) or been restricted to a small number of isolated grammatical structures (Adamec and Schaller).

Much of the original research for this work was carried out in conjunction with the Contemporary Russian Language Analysis Project at the University of Essex and many of the examples quoted are from a selection of the project's texts. The remaining examples quoted in this work are taken primarily from Soviet literature and newspapers.

PART I

GENERAL PRINCIPLES

1. FUNCTIONS OF ELEMENT ORDER

The factors underlying the order of elements can broadly be placed under three heads: contextual; grammatical; stylistic.

A. *Contextual*

Language can be examined from many points of view. One can examine the grammatical structures employed by a language and divide them up into sentences, clauses, groups, etc., as is explained in section 2 of part I. One can, on the other hand, examine language from the point of view of the information which it communicates. It is this kind of examination which will be termed 'contextual'.

Such information can be classified as either *new* or *given*. The 'new' information (or simply the 'new') is the essential piece of information which has caused the sentence to be uttered; it is the aim of the utterance. The 'given' information (or simply the 'given') is information which is incidental to the main purpose of the utterance. Its purpose is often cohesive, that is to help a text to hang together. An utterance does not necessarily contain a 'given' but always contains a 'new'. These two terms cover the whole of the utterance—that which is not given must be new and vice versa.

It is not intended that given and new should be correlated with known and unknown information respectively. It may frequently be the case that the categories coincide, as in the following example:

Звенéла за бóртом водá, и звон э́тот был похóж на звук бегýщего, весёлого, никогдá не умолкáющего ручья́. (Kazakov, На óстрове)	There was a ringing sound overboard and this ringing was like that of a stream running, gay, never silent.

In the second clause the given is 'звон э́тот'. We already know from the preceding clause that there was a ringing sound; the new in this second clause is the description of this ringing, which is not known to the reader.

In this next example, however, all the pieces of information are unknown:

19 декабря́ в Кремлé Н. В. Подгóрный вручи́л óрден Лéнина Л. И. Брéжневу. (Прáвда, 20.12.66, abbreviated)	On 19 December in the Kremlin N. V. Podgorny conferred the Order of Lenin on L. I. Brezhnev.

One does not know beforehand either when and where the action is taking place or what the action is. However, clearly, the time and place act as given and the action itself as new, because the article is not concerned with stressing the time or place but with the conferment itself. The time and place are incidental pieces of background information and not necessary to the understanding of the article.

The division into given and new is a very broad one and any application of this type of contextual analysis to the examination of element order requires a further subdivision of the new into two parts—into *essential* and *non-essential* new. The essential new is the central core of the new, the word(s) within the new of the greatest significance. The remainder of the new is non-essential. Such a division of the new is usually only necessary when the new covers more than one grammatical element.

In the following example the three types of information can be clearly seen:

Пришёл с по́ля хозя́ин. Уста́лый, он присе́л отдохну́ть на ствол па́льмы, сби́той взрывно́й волно́й бо́мбы.
(Изве́стия, 31.11.66)

The owner came from the field. Tired, he sat down for a rest on the trunk of a palm tree, which had been shattered by the shock wave of a bomb.

In the second sentence one is not concerned with the person who sat down (given) but with the fact that he sat down for a rest (non-essential new) and especially with the place where he sat down for this rest (essential new).

So far the information in the utterance has been divided into given and new, and new has been further subdivided into non-essential and essential new. These contextual elements are most frequently found in the following order: given (if present) precedes new and, when it is found necessary to subdivide the new, the non-essential new precedes the essential new:

GIVEN — NEW
non-essential—essential

Such is the order in all the examples quoted above.

In utterances having a high degree of emphasis, often emotionally coloured, the order of the essential and non-essential new is reversed, while that of the given and new remains unchanged:

GIVEN — NEW
essential—non-essential

This order will be termed 'emphatic' and is commonly found in exclamations and in the spoken language. It is also less frequently found in the written language where special emphasis is being placed on the essential new.

This order of given—essential new—non-essential new is found in the following example:

Но́вая па́ртия и здесь идёт я́вно про́тив тече́ния.
(Пра́вда, 4.11.66)

The new party is even here going clearly against the current.

The reader is not so much interested in the fact that it is the new party (given) (subject of the whole article from which this sentence comes) which is going against the current (non-essential new) but in the fact that it is even here (essential new) that it is going against the current.

Very frequently in emphatic order no given is present; the order is simply essential new preceding non-essential new. This is the case in the following example, where the emphasis is on the soldiers, because it is only in them that the author sees real courageous men:

То́лько в солда́тах ви́дит он настоя́щих и му́жественных люде́й.
(Изв АН СССР, сер лит и яз, vol. 24, 1965)

It is only in the soldiers that he sees real and courageous men.

Note the special construction which English uses to reflect this emphasis.

In utterances with emphatic order the essential new is often marked by the presence of such emphatic words as и, и́менно, да́же, то́лько; this is the case in the last two examples.

Even in utterances with a non-emphatic order the degree of emphasis may vary, depending on two factors: (i) The frequency of occurrence of a given order of grammatical elements. The more frequently a particular order occurs, the less emphatic it is; the more rarely such an order is found, the greater is the degree of emphasis attached to it. One finds that, although a number of orders of grammatical elements is grammatically possible and contextually justifiable, one will be more frequent than the rest. Such an order will have the least degree of emphasis. For example, the order subject—verb—object will have the least degree of emphasis, being the most frequent. (ii) The presence of emphatic words. Such words are commonly present in emphatic order (see above). They may, however, also be present in non-emphatic order, where they serve to increase the emphasis on the essential new.

The following invented examples will demonstrate how the degree of emphasis in an utterance is affected by alterations in element order and by the presence or absence of emphatic words.

(1) Пётр ненави́дел Ива́на. — Peter hated Ivan.
(2) Ива́на ненави́дел Пётр. — Ivan was hated by Peter.
(3) Ива́на ненави́дел и Пётр. — Ivan was hated by Peter as well.
(4) Пётр Ива́на ненави́дел. — Peter *hated* Ivan.
(5) Ненави́дел Ива́на Пётр. — It was Peter who hated Ivan.
(6) И Пётр ненави́дел Ива́на. — Even Peter hated Ivan.

The shifts of emphasis are as follows. (1) is a completely non-emphatic statement of fact: given—Peter; non-essential new—hated; essential new—Ivan. (2) has a somewhat greater emphasis, because it occurs less frequently: given—Ivan; non-essential new—hated; essential new—Peter. (3) has the same contextual analysis as (2) with the exception that greater emphasis is attached to the essential new. (4) and (5) are much more rarely found and thus much more emphatic. They demand special contexts. (4) might be found in a discussion of the personal relationship between Peter and Ivan when one person emphatically declares that Peter did not like Ivan; in fact, he positively hated him. Here we have: given—Peter; non-essential new—Ivan; essential new—hated. (5) might be found in a discussion of who hated Ivan. In other words, it is known that someone hated him. This sentence establishes that it was Peter: given—hated Ivan; new—Peter. In (6) we find the emphatic order of contextual elements. 'Peter', the essential new, precedes the non-essential new 'hated Ivan'.

Notice that English has a fixed element order, maintaining the order: subject—verb—object in all the translations. It conveys the shifts of emphasis by such means as the use of a passive construction, the use of the 'it was Peter who' construction, etc.

So far all the examples have illustrated the order of elements in the structure of the clause (clause elements). Given and new may also be applied to the order of clauses in the sentence and, to a lesser extent, to that of individual words in groups.

Но Кудря́вцев сказа́л, что прокуро́ра на акти́ве не́ было. (Chakovsky, Неве́ста)

But Kudryavtsev said that the judge was not at work.

Given—'Кудря́вцев'; non-essential new—'сказа́л'; essential new—'что прокуро́ра на акти́ве не́ было'. This does not mean that the dependent clause itself cannot be divided into given and new. Within the dependent clause the following is the contextual analysis: given—'прокуро́ра'; non-essential new—'на акти́ве'; essential new—'не́ было'. In other words, one has the following pattern:

GIVEN—NON-ESSENTIAL NEW—ESSENTIAL NEW
given—non-ess. new—ess. new

In the following sentence the two adjectives at the end act as essential new; the non-essential new is 'наро́д', the given is 'пе́вчие'. Here the order of individual words and not clauses or clause elements is being determined by their contextual function:

Пе́вчие — наро́д пья́ный и малоинте-ре́сный. (Gorky, В лю́дях)

Singers are a race of drunkards and of little interest.

B. *Grammatical*

Grammatical restrictions on element order in Russian are not as strict as in English, where the function of an element is most frequently determined by its position. Thus in statements in English the subject is distinguished from the object by the fact that it precedes instead of follows the verb. In Russian the function of an element is determined by inflexion rather than the position of the elements relative to each other. This leaves Russian greater scope for element order to express the contextual distinctions discussed above.

This does not mean that no grammatical rules determining element order exist. For example, words in the genitive case follow the noun which they modify; co-ordinating and subordinating conjunctions stand at the beginning of their clause, etc. The detailed grammatical rules determining element order will not be discussed at this point but later in part II.

C. *Stylistic*

The third factor affecting element order is stylistic. There are occasions when different element orders are possible and yet the grammatical and contextual analyses remain the same. Such occasions are comparatively rare. It is only in this limited way that element order in Russian can be said to be truly free. Reference will be made to such cases of free stylistic variation in part II.

2. GRAMMATICAL ANALYSIS

As stated above, no satisfactory and consistent grammatical analysis of Russian is widely accepted. This has made it necessary to sketch the analysis used for determining the structures to be examined in part II. The categories used often differ from the traditional ones only in their names; what is innovatory in the system is the way in which all the sections of the analysis are related to each other.

Exemplification has been largely avoided in this section because a large number of examples will be found when the order of the elements is discussed in part II.

The analysis has been carried out in accordance with the theoretical framework of M. A. K. Halliday (see bibliography). In terms of Halliday's grammatical theory, the grammar of a language is made up of units, which are hierarchically ordered on a 'scale of rank' (or 'rank scale'). For Russian five such units are needed: sentence; clause; group; word; morpheme. According to the theory sentences consist of clauses, clauses of groups, etc. Sentences never consist directly of groups, clauses

11

never consist directly of words, etc. Clauses may, however, contain in their structure clauses and not, as is expected, groups. In the following example the clause 'улучшить качество удобрений' (to improve the quality of the manures) is analysed as a clause, functioning (as subject) where a nominal group usually functions:

Особенно важно улучшить качество удобрений.
(Известия, 11.11.66)

It is especially important to improve the quality of the manures.

A clause functioning in this way is said to be 'rank-shifted', i.e. it has been shifted down the rank scale.

Similarly, when groups contain in their structure groups or clauses, and not, as is expected, words, such clauses and groups are also termed 'rank-shifted'. In the following example the clause 'по которой въехали в село' (along which they rode into the village) is rank-shifted:

Улица, по которой въехали в село, пересекается другой.
(Kozhevnikov, Живая вода)

The street along which they rode into the village is crossed by another.

In the following example the group 'моего брата' (of my brother) is rank-shifted:

книга моего брата

the book of my brother

A. *Sentence structure*

Sentences consist of clauses. These clauses are either independent clauses or they are dependent. Independent clauses are called *alpha* clauses; those clauses dependent on an alpha clause are called *beta* clauses, those clauses dependent on a beta clause are called *gamma* clauses, etc.

Dependent clauses (beta, gamma...) are of three kinds: conditioning; reported; additioning.

Conditioning clauses are often called in traditional terminology 'adverbial clauses' and like adverbial clauses are subclassified on semantic grounds into: time; manner; cause; aim; condition; concession; result; contrast. Note that place clauses have been omitted from the above classification. In this work they are considered to be either rank-shifted or additioning clauses (see below).

Conditioning clauses are also classified according to the element which binds them to the independent clause. Such elements are: binding adjunct; predicator—gerund, infinitive, imperative; subject; complement; adjunct. (The meaning of these terms is explained in sub-section B, 'Clause structure'.)

Reported clauses correspond to the traditional categories of indirect

12

statement, question and command and they are likewise subclassified into statement, question and command.

Additioning clauses are those which are added to the alpha clause without in any way limiting its applicability. They are subclassified into: non-defining; parenthetic.

Non-defining clauses embrace relative clauses and 'pseudo-relative' clauses of time and place (i.e. those where the conjunction can be replaced by a relative word) which give additional information about their antecedent but do not limit its applicability in any way. Compare:

Тот человéк, с котóрым я разговáривал, живёт в Москвé.	That man I was talking to lives in Moscow.
Ивáнов, с котóрым я разговáривал, живёт в Москвé.	Ivanov, to whom I was talking, lives in Moscow.

The first sentence contains a defining relative clause ('с котóрым я разговáривал'), which is classed as rank-shifted. This limits the applicability of the antecedent in the same way as an adjective does. The second sentence contains a non-defining relative clause ('с котóрым я разговáривал'), which is classed as a beta additioning clause. This merely gives additional gratuitous information about the antecedent, without in any way limiting its applicability.

Parenthetic clauses are those clauses inserted into a sentence which either quote the source of a statement:

Он, *как говоря́т лётчики*, соблазни́лся лёгкой ди́чью... (Polevoy, Пóвесть о настоя́щем человéке)	He, as the pilots put it, was enticed by easy game...

or contain a comment by the author on the information in the alpha clause:

Не бýду касáться егó биогрáфии — сам он, *наскóлько пóмню*, не óчень-то люби́л говори́ть об истóках... (Литератýрная газéта, 14.6.67)	I won't concern myself with his biography—he himself, as far as I remember, did not very much like to talk of his origins...

or have a cohesive function:

Что касáется лири́ческой прóзы, то я хотéл бы присоедини́ться к Л. Кря́чко, отмéтившей реша́ющее значéние сáмой ли́чности áвтора в э́том жáнре. (Литератýрная газéта, 31.1.68)	As far as lyric prose is concerned, I should like to join L. Kryachko, who has noted the decisive significance of the personality of the author in this genre.

(The parenthetic clauses have been italicised by the author of this work.)

B. *Clause structure*

Four elements of clause structure are distinguished: subject (S); predicator (P); complement (C); adjunct (A). (The letters in brackets are mnemonics which will be used throughout this work.)

S, P, C and A are labels attached to one or more groups, dependent on their function in the clause. The terms 'nominal', 'verbal', 'adverbial' and 'preposition-plus-complement'[1] groups refer to the class of group, irrespective of their function in the clause. There is usually a close correspondence between class and function but never an exact one. Thus predicators are usually realised by verbal groups but this is by no means always the case (see below).

Subject

'Subject' is used in the traditional meaning of the term. It is most frequently realised by a nominal group in the nominative case. It may also be in the genitive case in clauses containing a negative verbal group:

Его фамилии просто не оказалось в списке... (Chakovsky, Невеста)	His name was simply not on the list...

or a quantitative nominal group:

Их было очень много. (Chakovsky, Невеста)	There were lots and lots of them.

The subject may also be realised by a rank-shifted clause:

Алексею стало стыдно, что он увлёкся лёгкой добычей. (Polevoy, Повесть о настоящем человеке)	Aleksey was ashamed that he had been carried away by easy prey.

Predicator

The predicator is usually realised by a verbal group. It may, however, also be realised by a non-verbal group such as надо, необходимо, нужно, должен, можно, нельзя. The predicator may consist of two (or, rarely, more) groups. One will be a verbal group in the infinitive, the other a finite part of such verbs as хотеть(ся), мочь, приходиться, удаваться or one of the non-verbal groups mentioned above. The two groups are then said to be *in phase* and the predicator is termed *phased*.

Phased predicators should not be confused with compound verbal

---

[1] Complement as in 'preposition-plus-complement' signifies the word(s) dependent on a preposition and should not be confused with the element of clause structure 'complement'.

groups. These are verbal groups consisting of more than one word—a main verb (in the infinitive or passive participle form) and an auxiliary (usually part of the verb быть).

The following two clauses illustrate the difference. The first has a compound verbal group, the second a phased P:

Сл бу́дет забо́титься о́бо мне.	He will be looking after me.
Ему́ на́до забо́титься о́бо мне.	He has to look after me.

Complement

Two types of complement are distinguished: extensive (C^E); intensive (C^I).

The *extensive complement*, for the most part, corresponds to the traditional category of object. Three classes of extensive complement are distinguished.

C^{E1} corresponds to the traditional category of direct object and is usually realised by a nominal group in the accusative case. It may also be in the genitive (with such verbs as каса́ться, боя́ться or, frequently, after negative verbal groups), dative (with such verbs as помога́ть, позволя́ть), or instrumental case (with such verbs as по́льзоваться, пра́вить).

C^{E2} corresponds to the traditional category of indirect object and is realised by a nominal group in the dative case. It is distinguished from C^{E1} in the following ways: it can be found with passive verbal groups as well as with active ones; with active verbal groups there is the possibility, though not the necessity, of the presence of a C^{E1}.

C^{E3} has no corresponding category in English and is realised by a nominal group in the dative case. It is found with such predicators as приходи́ться, хоте́ться, нра́виться, на́до, ну́жно, мо́жно. It is the *logical* subject of the clause, but cannot be classed as the *grammatical* subject, because a grammatical subject may also appear in the same clause, as, for example, with the verb нра́виться.

The following clause illustrates the three classes of extensive complement:

Ему́ (C^{E3}) на́до переда́ть отцу́ (C^{E2}) письмо́ (C^{E1}).	He has to give his father the letter.

The *intensive complement* (C^I) corresponds to the traditional category of complement and is found with such verbs as быть, каза́ться, ока́зываться, явля́ться. It is most frequently realised by a nominal group in the instrumental case, or the nominative case with the present tense 'zero form' and, very frequently, also the past tense of the verb быть.

In all these cases the intensive complement refers to the subject. It may also refer to the C^{E1}. Such intensive complements will be labelled C^{IC}. It is illustrated in the following example:

В. Днепро́в предложи́л счита́ть рома́н самостоя́тельным ро́дом иску́сства. (Литерату́рная газе́та, 6.10.66)	V. Dneprov proposed that the novel should be considered an independent form of art.

Here the intensive complement ('самостоя́тельным ро́дом иску́сства') refers to the C^{E1} ('рома́н'). C^{IC} is frequently found with such verbs as счита́ть, рассма́тривать and may be realised by a nominal group in the instrumental (less frequently nominative) or in the accusative case following как:

Руково́дство людьми́ Никола́й рассма́тривал как тя́жкое бре́мя. (Chakovsky, Неве́ста)	Nikolay considered the guidance of men to be a heavy burden.

Adjunct

Two classes of adjunct are distinguished. The first one (A^1) comprises, on the one hand, the purely grammatical functional words: (i) linking adjuncts—known in traditional terminology as co-ordinating conjunctions; (ii) binding adjuncts—known in traditional terminology as subordinating conjunctions; (iii) interrogative adjuncts—usually realised by ли; and, on the other, parenthetic adjuncts. These adjuncts perform one of three functions: (i) they pass comment on the information contained in the clause—e.g. вероя́тно, мо́жет быть; (ii) they quote the source of a statement—e.g. по-мо́ему, согла́сно Толсто́му; (iii) they provide a loose cohesive link with the previous sentence—e.g. поэ́тому, к тому́ же.

The second class (A^2) is classified in two ways. First, on semantic grounds into: time; manner; degree; place—direction; place—position; cause; aim; condition; concession; agency. Secondly, according to the class of group: adverbial group; preposition-plus-complement group; nominal group—accusative, genitive, instrumental.

The following two examples contain a preposition-plus-complement adjunct of time and a preposition-plus-complement adjunct of place (in the first example), and an adverbial adjunct of manner (in the second):

Че́рез не́сколько часо́в начнёт вечере́ть и в за́падных города́х. (Изве́стия, 1.12.66)	In a few hours it will begin to get dark even in the towns in the west.
Кита́йцы дово́льно легко́ мо́гут прокопа́ть подзе́мный ход в О́дензе. (Paustovsky, Ска́зочник)	The Chinese could quite easily dig an underground passage to Odense.

c. *Group structure*

Nominal and adverbial groups consist of main words or *heads* (H) and those words dependent on the head (whether preceding or following it) or *modifiers* (M); words dependent on modifiers are termed *submodifiers* (MM), etc. Adverbial groups will not be further subclassified.

Nominal group modifiers are further subclassified as follows:

(i)   *Adjectival*

(ii) *Deictic*

This class embraces possessive (мой, твой, его...), quantitative (мно́го, ма́ло, не́сколько...), demonstrative (тако́й, э́тот, тот...) and serial words (друго́й, ино́й...).

(iii) *Numeral*

(iv) *Rank-shifted nominal group*

The last is a case of a group acting as an element of group structure and therefore rank-shifted (see p. 12). It may be in one of three cases: genitive, dative or instrumental, as illustrated in the following example:

обуче́ние ру́сскому языку́ иностра́н-цев сове́тскими преподава́телями	the teaching of Russian to foreigners by Soviet teachers

(v)   *Rank-shifted preposition-plus-complement group*

This once again is a case of a group acting as an element of group structure. It is illustrated in the following example:

его́ подхо́д к э́тому вопро́су	his approach to this problem

(vi) *Rank-shifted clause*

This is a clause acting as modifier in the nominal group. It may be a defining relative clause (see the discussion on beta additioning clauses above on p. 13) or a clause of the following type:

Зада́ча заключа́ется в том, что́бы пра́вильно организова́ть рабо́ту. (Ushakov, Толко́вый слова́рь ру́сского языка́)	The problem is to organise the work properly.

(vii) *Adverb*

This is a comparatively rare class of modifier and is most frequently found with adverbs of place-direction:

поворо́т нале́во (Пра́вила движе́ния, 1965)	a turn to the left

(viii) *Parenthetic word*

This performs the same functions as the parenthetic A[1] but refers to one part of the clause and not to the clause as a whole. The two parenthetic words in the following example are italicised (by the author of this work):

Подпо́лье бы́ло озабо́чено, *во-пе́рвых*, уча́стью това́рищей в тюрьма́х, *во-вторы́х*, нараста́ющими собы́тиями по дере́вням Подлу́жья.

(Bakhmet'yev, У поро́га)

The underground was concerned, first, about the fate of their comrades in prison secondly, about the increase in incidents around the villages of Podluzh'ye.

One important feature of the above analysis is that one and the same set of words can perform a different function dependent on whether it is an element of the clause or the group. Compare these two clauses:

Он подошёл к до́му неожи́данно.

He approached the house unexpectedly.

Его́ подхо́д к до́му был неожи́данным.

His approach to the house was unexpected.

In the first clause 'к до́му' is an adjunct of place—an element of clause structure. In the second it is a rank-shifted group acting as modifier to 'подхо́д'—an element of nominal group structure.

PART II

ORDER OF ELEMENTS

1. ORDER OF CLAUSES

This section is concerned with the order of alpha and beta clauses in the sentence. Three positions for a beta clause are possible: preceding the alpha clause; following the alpha clause; interrupting the alpha clause. When a beta clause interrupts an alpha clause, it is usually found following a complete clause element. Apart from this, there is no restriction on its position interrupting the alpha clause. The references in this section to beta clauses apply also to gamma clauses dependent on beta clauses, etc.

The beta clause has one of two contextual functions in the sentence: (i) it may act as essential new to the non-essential new and given in the alpha clause; (ii) it may act as given to the essential and non-essential new in the alpha clause. Within the beta clause the given and new are distinguished quite independently of the contextual function of the clause in the sentence (see p. 10).

On the other hand, the alpha and beta clauses may be contextually quite independent of each other. Within the alpha and beta clauses one can distinguish a given and a new, but it is not possible to distinguish a given and new for the sentence as a whole.

A. *Conditioning*

Beta conditioning clauses precede or follow the alpha clause more frequently than they interrupt it. There is, however, considerable variation between the different classes of conditioning clause. The contextual role of the clause in the sentence also varies quite considerably from one class of conditioning clause to another. Each class of conditioning clause will be examined separately, taking account of the following two factors: (i) the contextual role of the clause in the three positions in the sentence; (ii) the frequency of occurrence in each of these three positions.

The percentages quoted in this subsection are based on an examination of the Essex Russian Language Project's texts.

(a) *Time*

Beta conditioning clauses of time, when preceding or interrupting the alpha clause, play no contextual role in the sentence: they are contextually independent of each other. Interrupting the alpha clause, they attract more emphasis than when preceding it. Compare:

Когда́ она́ умрёт, на́до бу́дет разве́ять её пе́пел с самолёта...
(Литерату́рная газе́та, 14.6.67)

When she dies, we shall have to scatter her ashes from a plane...

with:

Фома́ Зо́рькин, вступи́в в Комсомо́л, начина́ет борьбу́ с отцо́м и ма́терью.
(Изв АН СССР, сер лит и яз, vol. 24, 1965)

Foma Zor'kin, having become a member of the Komsomol, began a struggle with his father and mother.

When following the alpha clause, time clauses which are bound by a binding adjunct act as essential new to the given and non-essential new in the alpha clause:

Челове́к начина́ет про́бовать эксперименти́ровать, когда́ возника́ет потре́бность и ве́ра в возмо́жность измене́ния.
(Изв АН СССР, сер лит и яз, vol. 24, 1965)

A man begins to try to experiment, when there arises a need and a belief in the possibility of change.

When following the alpha clause, time clauses which are bound by a gerund may have two contextual analyses. When 'replacing' a clause bound by a binding adjunct such as когда́, до того́ как, по́сле того́ как, the beta time clause bound by a gerund, like these clauses, acts as essential new to the non-essential new and given in the alpha clause:

Крейн написа́л «А́лый знак до́блести», ни ра́зу не побыва́в на теа́тре вое́нных де́йствий.
(Изв АН СССР, сер лит и яз, vol. 24, 1965)

Crane wrote *The Red Badge of Courage*, never once having been in the theatre of war.

When 'replacing' two co-ordinated clauses, the beta time clause bound by a gerund, like these clauses, has an independent contextual analysis:

На ра́зных эта́пах своего́ истори́ческого пути́ сове́тская поэ́зия обнару́живала ра́зные характе́рные осо́бенности, остава́ясь при э́том поэ́зией революцио́нной.
(Литерату́рная газе́та, 27.9.66)

At various stages of its historical path Soviet poetry revealed various characteristic properties, while still remaining the poetry of the revolution.

The frequency of occurrence preceding, following or interrupting the alpha clause depends on whether the time clause is bound by a binding adjunct or a gerund.

When bound by a binding adjunct, the beta time clause precedes the alpha clause on 60% of occasions, follows on 33% and interrupts on only 7%. The following examples illustrate each of the three positions in the sentence—preceding, following and interrupting the alpha clause, respectively:

Когда́ кома́ндующий фло́том Са́блин о́тдал прика́з гото́виться к неме́дленной эвакуа́ции, миноно́сцы отказа́ли его́ вы́полнить.
(Paustovsky, Чёрное мо́ре)

When the commander of the fleet Sablin gave the order to prepare for speedy evacuation, the torpedo boats refused to carry it out.

Да и литерату́ра не мо́жет ждать, когда́ все перево́дчики ста́нут полигло́тами.
(Литерату́рная газе́та, 28.8.67)

But literature cannot wait until all translators become polyglots.

Худо́жник, пре́жде чем писа́ть карти́ну, набра́сывает этю́ды.
(Granin, Иска́тели)

The artist, before painting a picture, draws sketches.

When bound by a gerund, the beta time clause follows the alpha clause on 49 % of occasions, precedes on 27 % and interrupts on 24 %. The following examples illustrate the three positions in the sentence—following, preceding and interrupting the alpha clause, respectively:

Чита́тель вы́нужден суди́ть об у́ровне це́лой литерату́ры, приходя́ подча́с к безотра́дным о ней сужде́ниям.
(Литерату́рная газе́та, 28.8.67)

The reader is forced to assess the level of a whole literature, forming at times a very unhappy opinion of it.

Чита́я расска́зы В. Лихоно́сова, пережива́ешь беду́ до́брой Маре́и.
(Литерату́рная газе́та, 22.11.66)

Reading the stories of V. Likhonosov, you experience the misfortune of dear Mareya.

Ча́ще всего́, прикры́в дверь ку́хни, она́ говори́т о том, что Воло́дя пло́хо ест.
(Литерату́рная газе́та, 14.6.67)

Most frequently, having pushed the kitchen door to, she tells you that Volodya has a poor appetite.

(b) Manner

Beta clauses of manner most frequently follow the alpha clause on which they are dependent. In this position the beta clause is contextually independent of the alpha clause. It may be bound by как or any of its synonyms, meaning 'just as':

Путь Шо́лохова в литерату́ру — необыча́йно сло́жный, как у вся́кого большо́го худо́жника сло́жен проце́сс духо́вного обогаще́ния ли́чности.
(Изв АН СССР, сер лит и яз, vol. 24, 1965)

Sholokhov's path into literature is unusually complex, just as with any great artist the process of spiritual enrichment of the personality is complex.

On the other hand, beta clauses of manner may be bound by (как) бу́дто or any of its synonyms, meaning 'as if':

Он идёт бы́стро и уве́ренно, бу́дто не раз уже́ ходи́л здесь.
(V. Nekrasov, В око́пах Сталингра́да)

He walks quickly and with assurance, as if he had been here many times before.

21

Beta clauses of manner may also precede or interrupt the alpha clause. In these positions in the sentence, they are often in a reduced form, containing besides the binding adjunct only one other element; the remaining elements are omitted or 'deleted'. These clauses stand after or before the element in the alpha clause with which the reduced beta clause is being contrasted:

Мне, как и мно́гим писа́телям, претя́т возника́ющие иногда́ спо́ры об идеа́льном геро́е.
(Литерату́рная газе́та, 28.6.67)

I, just like many writers, am sickened by the disputes which arise from time to time about the ideal hero.

Как и литерату́ре, кри́тике то́же необходи́мо многообра́зие фо́рмы.
(Литерату́рная газе́та, 3.12.66)

Just like literature, so does criticism need a multiplicity of forms.

(c) *Cause*

Beta clauses of cause preceding the alpha clause usually have an independent contextual analysis:

Так как на селе́ не нашло́сь помеще́-ния, могу́щего вмести́ть всех собра́в-шихся, собра́ние состоя́лось на от-кры́том во́здухе.   (Laptev, Заря́)

Because there was not a place in the village capable of holding the whole gathering, the meeting was held in the open air.

Following the alpha clause, when the binding adjunct is realised by и́бо or поско́льку, the beta clause of cause also has an independent contextual analysis:

На э́тот вопро́с мне хо́чется отве́тить, и́бо он уже́ затра́гивает существо́ пробле́мы.
(Литерату́рная газе́та, 27.9.66)

This question I want to answer, as it already touches on the essence of the problem.

Otherwise the beta clause of cause following the alpha clause acts as essential new to the given and non-essential new in the alpha clause:

Маши́ны засвети́ли фа́ры, потому́ что в лесу́ уже́ стемне́ло.
(Nikolayeva, Жа́тва)

The cars had switched on their head-lights, because it had already grown dark in the forest.

Clauses bound by и́бо always follow the alpha clause, those bound by потому́ что almost always do. When clauses of the latter type precede the alpha clause, they act as essential new in emphatic order, preceding the non-essential new in the alpha clause:

И́менно потому́ что кни́га самого́ Н. Шамоты́ постро́ена на э́тих при́н-ципах, она́ ста́ла одни́м из по́длинных обрете́ний сего́дняшней кри́тики.
(Литерату́рная газе́та, 3.12.66)

It is just because the book of N. Shamota is constructed on these principles that it has become one of the real finds of con-temporary criticism.

Clauses bound by the binding adjunct поско́льку precede or follow the alpha clause equally frequently with no difference in emphasis:

Все идут учиться, поскольку есть интерес к знаниям. (Ushakov, Толковый словарь русского языка)	Everyone goes to study, since there is an interest in knowledge.
Поскольку ты согласен, я не возражаю. (Ushakov, Толковый словарь русского языка)	Since you are agreeable, I do not object.

Clauses bound by the binding adjunct так как usually follow the alpha clause but may also precede, as in the first example of this subsection.

(d) Aim

Following the alpha clause, the beta clause of aim acts as essential new to the given and non-essential new in the alpha clause:

Лукашин встряхнулся, чтобы ноша удобнее легла на плече. (Panova, Кружилиха)	Lukashin gave himself a shake, so that the burden should lie more comfortably on his shoulder.

Preceding the alpha clause, the beta clause of aim has an independent contextual analysis:

Ведь для того, чтобы быть действительно свободным, искусство, прежде всего, должно быть искусством. (Литературная газета, 3.12.66)	In order to be really free, art, above all, must be art.

When bound by an infinitive alone, the beta clause of aim always follows the alpha clause:

Приходили люди с заводов прочитать свои первые стихи. (Изв АН СССР, сер лит и яз, vol. 24, 1965)	People came from the factories to read their first poems.

When bound by a binding adjunct, the beta clause of aim follows the alpha clause on two out of every three occasions.

(e) Condition

Following the alpha clause, the beta clause of condition acts as essential new to the non-essential new and given in the alpha clause:

Было бы неестественно, если бы художественное творчество в этих условиях не выявило новых тенденций. (Литературная газета, 27.9.66)	It would be unnatural if artistic creativity in these conditions did not show fresh tendencies.

Preceding the alpha clause, the beta clause of condition has an independent contextual analysis:

Éсли же произведéния и рассмáтриваются, то обы́чно э́то тóлько «Мэ́гги — дéвушка с у́лицы» и «Áлый знак дóблести.»
(Изв АН СССР, сер лит и яз, vol. 24, 1965)

Even if his works are examined at all, it is usually only *Maggie, the Girl from the Streets* and *The Red Badge of Courage*.

Изучáя твóрчество Крéйна в цéлом, мы мóжем утверждáть, что реалисти́ческие тендéнции торжествовáли над чертáми натурали́зма.
(Изв АН СССР, сер лит и яз, vol. 24, 1965)

Studying the work of Crane as a whole, we can state that the realistic tendencies triumphed over the features of naturalism.

Interrupting the alpha clause, beta clauses of condition also have an independent contextual analysis. In such cases the clause is emphasized:

Мысль, éсли онá не стáла фóрмой дéятельности, ещё не свобóдная мысль.
(Литератýрная газéта, 3.12.66)

A thought, if it has not become a form of activity, is not as yet a free thought.

When bound by a binding adjunct, the beta clause of condition precedes the alpha clause on 70% of occasions; it follows the alpha clause on 21% of occasions and interrupts on 9%. When bound by a gerund, the beta clause of condition precedes the alpha clause on 57% of occasions; it follows the alpha clause on 28% of occasions and interrupts on 15%.

When bound by an imperative verbal group, the beta clause of condition always precedes the alpha clause:

Доведи́сь мне писáть егó зáново, я снóва по глáвной принципиáльной ли́нии — реши́л бы егó так же.
(Литератýрная газéта, 14.6.67)

If I had to write it again, I should once again have followed the same basic principles.

(f) Concession

Whatever its position in the clause, the beta clause of concession has an independent contextual analysis. Clauses bound by the binding adjunct хотя́ have a tendency to follow the alpha clause:

Я вы́пустил ужé три кни́жки расскáзов, хотя́ины́е из них в итóге достáвили мне бóльше огорчéний, чем рáдостей...
(Литератýрная газéта, 14.6.67)

I have already published three books of stories, although some of them have in the end given me more worry than pleasure...

but they may also precede the alpha clause:

Хотя́ различ́ие в вóзрасте бы́ло ничтóжным, рáзница в восприя́тии перелóмной эпóхи, обознáченной XX съéздом, былá кудá бóлее значи́тельной.
(Литератýрная газéта, 22.11.66)

Although the difference in age was insignificant, the difference in the perception of the epoch of crisis, marked by the 20th congress, was much more important.

Those clauses bound by a pronoun plus (бы) ни have a tendency to precede the alpha clause:

Ско́лько бы ни писа́лось о жела́тель- | However much has been written about
ности переводи́ть непосре́дственно с | the desirability of translating directly
оригина́ла, мину́я подстро́чник, мы | from the original, avoiding the word for
всё ещё далеки́ от э́того идеа́ла… | word translation, we are still far from
(Литерату́рная газе́та, 28.6.67) | this ideal…

but such clauses may also follow the alpha clause:

У него́ ничего́ не кле́илось, что бы он | Nothing of his ever got off the ground,
ни предпринима́л. | whatever he undertook.
(Fedin, Необыкнове́нное ле́то)

According to the Academy Grammar, the binding adjuncts пусть and пуска́й are always found in beta clauses of concession preceding the alpha clause. It quotes:

Пуска́й ты у́мер, но в пе́снях сме́лых и | Though you have died, yet in the songs of
си́льных ду́хом, Всегда́ ты бу́дешь | the bold and strong in spirit, you will
приме́ром до́брым… | always be a good example…
(Gorky, Пе́сня о со́коле)

However, such clauses are also found following the alpha clause:

Е́сли бы Ва́ля влюби́лась в хоро́шего, | If Valya had fallen in love with a good
де́льного ю́ношу,…что ж, я всё сде́лал | serious young man, well,…I would have
бы для сча́стья до́чери, пусть э́то и | done everything for my daughter's
обрекло́ меня́ на безра́достное оди- | happiness, even though this would have
но́чество. | condemned me to miserable loneliness.
(Chakovsky, Неве́ста)

Beta clauses of concession rarely interrupt the alpha clause. When they do so, they are emphasized:

А Ма́ша, хоть и стара́тельная была́ | Yet Masha, though she was a hard-
де́вушка, но хозя́йничать до́ма при- | working girl, took a long time to get used
вы́кла неторопли́во. | to looking after the house.
(Laptev, Заря́)

(g) Result

Beta clauses of result always follow the alpha clause and act as essential new to the given and non-essential new in the alpha clause:

Я на́чал чита́ть и зачита́лся так, что, к | I began to read and got so engrossed that
огорче́нию взро́слых, почти́ не обра- | to the annoyance of the grown-ups I paid
ти́л внима́ния на наря́дную ёлку. | hardly any attention to the decorated
(Paustovsky, Ска́зочник) | Christmas tree.

(h) Contrast

Beta clauses of contrast have an independent contextual analysis. Those bound by the binding adjunct тогда́ как always follow the alpha clause:

Сливáясь друг с дрýгом, онѝ покры́ли нéбо сзáди нас, тогдá как впередѝ онó бы́ло ещё я́сно.
(Gorky, Мой спýтник)

Merging with each other, they covered the sky behind us, whereas ahead of us it was still clear.

Those bound by the binding adjunct в то врéмя как may either precede:

В то врéмя как всё существó егó рвалóсь к бýрной и я́ростной защѝте, он застáвил себя́ мéдленным, незамéтным движéнием опустѝть рýку в кармáн...
(Polevoy, Пóвесть о настоя́щем человéке)

While all his being longed for a stormy and fierce defence, he forced himself slowly and inconspicuously to lower his hand into his pocket...

or follow the alpha clause:

Всю ночь над умéршем пел сверчóк, в то врéмя как мáльчик всю ночь проплáкал.
(Paustovsky, Скáзочник)

All night the cricket sang over the deceased, while the boy cried the whole night through.

TABLE 1

	Preceding alpha	Following alpha	Interrupting alpha
Time			
binding adjunct	1 I	2 EN	3 I
gerund	2 I	1 EN/I	2 I
Manner	2 I	1 I	2 I
Cause			
ибо	——	1 I	——
поскóльку	1 I	1 I	——
потомý что	3 EN	1 EN	——
так как	2 I	1 EN	——
Aim			
binding adjunct	2 I	1 EN	——
infinitive	——	1 EN	——
Condition			
binding adjunct	1 I	2 EN	3 I
gerund	1 I	2 EN	2 I
imperative	1 I	——	——
Concession			
бы ни	1 I	2 I	3 I
пусть, пускáй	1 I	2 I	——
хотя́	2 I	1 I	3 I
Result	——	1 EN	——
Contrast			
в то врéмя как	1· I	1 I	——
тогдá как	——	1 I	——

Table 1 summarises the frequency of occurrence of the various classes of beta clause in each of the three positions in the sentence and lists their contextual role in each position. The figures 1, 2 and 3 indicate the relative frequency of occurrence: 1—most frequent position; 2—less frequent position; 3—occurring comparatively rarely in this position. The letters indicate the contextual role: I—independent contextual role; EN—essential new; EN/I—essential new or independent contextual role. A dash indicates that the particular class of clause is not found in this sentence position.

B. *Reported*

Reported clauses most frequently follow the alpha clause. In this position they act as essential new to the given and non-essential new in the alpha clause. This applies to beta reported clauses which are statements:

Он говори́л, что ле́гче всего́ писа́л ска́зки... (Paustovsky, Ска́зочник)	He said that he had found fairy tales the easiest thing to write...

or questions:

Кудря́вцев...спроси́л Воло́дю, что тот ду́мает о своём бу́дущем... (Chakovsky, Неве́ста)	Kudryavtsev...asked Volodya what he thought about his future...

or commands:

Коренны́е интере́сы италья́нского рабо́чего кла́сса...настоя́тельно тре́буют, чтобы наступле́нию капиталисти́ческих монопо́лий бы́ло противопоста́влено еди́нство всех антиимпериалисти́ческих, демократи́ческих сил. (Пра́вда, 4.11.66)	The basic interests of the Italian working class...persistently demand that the advance of the capitalist monopolies should be opposed by the united anti-imperialist democratic forces.

Beta reported clauses may also precede the alpha clause. In this position they act as given to the non-essential and essential new in the alpha clause:

Что означа́ет чуде́сное схо́дство Ми́ши с Михаи́лом, гада́ть не прихо́дится. (Литерату́рная газе́та, 18.10.66)	What the remarkable likeness between Misha and Mikhail signifies, cannot even be conjectured.

This unusual order of alpha and beta reported clauses lays greater emphasis on the essential new in the sentence, which, as in the above example, is most frequently realised by the predicator in the alpha clause. Such an order is found only with 'meaningful' predicators and would be very unlikely to occur with a verb such as говори́ть. It is, therefore, extremely unlikely that the first example in this subsection on reported clauses could ever have the order of the clauses reversed.

c. *Additioning*

All beta additioning clauses, whether non-defining or parenthetic and whether preceding, following or interrupting the alpha clause, have a contextual function independent of that of the alpha clause.

(i) *Non-defining*

All non-defining clauses have their position in the sentence determined on purely grammatical grounds. They either follow or interrupt the alpha clause, coming immediately after that element in the alpha clause to which the non-defining clause refers. This applies to relative clauses:

Говоря́ о «но́вой, све́жей по́росли комсомо́льской литерату́ры...», А. Жа́ров на пе́рвое ме́сто выдвига́ет Шо́лохова, расска́зы кото́рого выделя́лись на страни́цах э́того журна́ла.	Talking of 'the new fresh offshoots of Komsomol literature...', A. Zharov puts in first place Sholokhov, whose stories have been featured on the pages of this magazine.
(Изв АН СССР, сер лит и яз, vol. 24, 1965)	
Поэ́зия Влади́мира Луговско́го, исто́ки кото́рой спервонача́лу, быть мо́жет, бы́ли то́же в каки́х-то кни́гах, сра́зу вы́рвалась на просто́р. На просто́р жи́зни...	The poetry of Vladimir Lugovskoy, the sources of which may originally also have been in certain books, has suddenly burst out into the open space. Into the open space of life...
(Литерату́рная газе́та, 14.6.67)	

and to 'pseudo-relative' clauses of time:

В бесконе́чном убыстре́нии полёта в бу́дущем, когда́ реакти́вные самолёты повыша́ют мо́щность мото́ров..., де́сять лет мо́гут стать це́лой эпо́хой...	In the endless acceleration of flight in the future, when jet planes increase the power of their engines..., ten years can become a whole epoch...
(Литерату́рная газе́та, 14.6.67)	

and place:

Сно́ва захо́дим в у́зкий кана́л, где с трудо́м мо́гут разойти́сь две ло́дки.	Once again we turn into a narrow channel, where two boats have difficulty in passing.
(Изве́стия, 31.11.66)	

Clauses bound by the relative word что which has an antecedent in the alpha clause behave in exactly the same way as other relative clauses:

Дове́рие, уважи́тельное отноше́ние к лю́дям, чего́ па́ртия тре́бует от ка́ждого руководи́теля, непреме́нно должны́ сочета́ться с са́мым взыска́тельным стро́гим контро́лем.	Trust, a respectful attitude to people, which the party demands of every leader, must without fail be combined with the most searching strict supervision.
(Изве́стия, 24.11.66)	

Those clauses which do not refer to one particular element in the alpha clause but to the clause as a whole, follow the alpha clause:

Тёплое уча́стие к нему́ [солда́ту] сочета́ется у Кре́йна с то́ном дру́жеского ю́мора и мя́гкой иро́нии, что вво́дит све́тлые тона́ в о́бщий драмати́ческий колори́т рома́на.
(Изв АН СССР, сер лит и яз, vol. 24, 1965)

A warm feeling of sympathy for him [the soldier] Crane combines with a tone of friendly humour and gentle irony, which introduces light shades into the general dramatic colouring of the novel.

(ii) Parenthetic

Two types of parenthetic clause are distinguished: (a) those which link a sentence to a preceding one stand initial in their sentence, preceding the alpha clause. These clauses may contain a 'gerund' such as говоря́ plus an adjunct of manner:

Да и Кудря́вцеву уже́ не хоте́лось руководи́ть таки́ми людьми́. Говоря́ открове́нно, он их поба́ивался...
(Chakovsky, Неве́ста)

But Kudryavtsev no longer wanted to lead such men. To speak quite candidly, he was a little frightened of them...

or, alternatively, they may start with the words: что каса́ется or что же до:

Что каса́ется Па́влика, то с ним пришло́сь-таки повози́ться.
(Katayev, Беле́ет па́рус одино́кий)

As far as Pavlik is concerned, we still have to take a lot of trouble with him.

Что же до конкре́тного реше́ния, при́нятого брига́дой, то оно́ сра́зу же обраста́ет вопро́сами...
(Литерату́рная газе́та, 18.10.66)

As far as the specific decision taken by the brigade is concerned, it is at once full of question marks...

and (b) those which quote the source of a statement or make a comment on the information found in the alpha clause are most frequently found preceding or interrupting the alpha clause:

Как мы узнаём из по́вести Н. Реу́та и М. Скря́бина «Брандва́хта»..., брига́да и впрямь была́ права́.
(Литерату́рная газе́та, 18.10.66)

As we know from the story by N. Reut and M. Skryabin *Firewatch*..., the brigade was indeed right.

Расска́зов, наско́лько я по́мню, он никогда́ не писа́л...
(Литерату́рная газе́та, 14.6.67)

Stories, as far as I remember, were something he never wrote...

but are also found following the alpha clause:

Литерату́ра мо́жет возвраща́ться к исхо́дному моме́нту, два́жды, три́жды, четы́режды анализи́ровать одну́ и ту же жи́зненную ситуа́цию, как э́то де́лает Достое́вский в «Бра́тьях Карама́зовых».
(Изв АН СССР, сер лит и яз, vol. 24, 1965)

Literature can return to the starting point, can analyse two, three, four times one and the same real life situation, as, for example, Dostoevsky does in *The Brothers Karamazov*.

There are no grammatical and no contextual reasons to distinguish one order of clauses from the other two. The following two sentences are just as grammatical and have the same distribution of emphasis as the one quoted above:

Насколько я помню, рассказов он никогда не писал.	As far as I remember, stories were something he never wrote.
Рассказов он никогда не писал, насколько я помню.	Stories were something he never wrote, as far as I remember.

The distinctions between the three sentence positions for the parenthetic additioning clause are stylistic. Interrupting the alpha clause, the beta clause has special application to the preceding element of the alpha clause; following the alpha clause, it gives the impression of being added as an afterthought, while preceding the alpha clause, it is stylistically neutral.

2. ORDER OF CLAUSE ELEMENTS

A. *Subject and predicator*

In most grammatical structures the subject (S) usually precedes the predicator (P); the order S—P occurs approximately three times[1] as frequently as the order P—S. The elements S and P may be found in the clause on their own:

Отец его умер. (Chakovsky, Невеста)	His father died.

or with other clause elements:

События последнего десятилетия захватывают все стороны нашего существования. (Литературная газета, 6.10.66)	The events of the last decade embrace all sides of our existence.
В течение 1894–5 гг. Крейн много путешествовал. (Изв АН СССР, сер лит и яз, vol. 24, 1965)	During 1894–5 Crane travelled a lot.

In all these examples with the order S—P S acts as given, and P as part or the whole of the new.

In the order P—S P usually acts as non-essential new and S as essential new:

---

[1] All the figures quoted in this section on the *Order of Clause Elements* are taken from an analysis of a selection of the Russian Language Project's texts, supplemented by texts from Soviet literature and newspapers.

В э́то вре́мя...показа́лся высо́кий и о́чень худо́й челове́к в чёрном. (Paustovsky, Ска́зочник)	At this time...there appeared a tall and very thin man in black.

S may also follow P when both S and P act as non-essential new and a following element acts as essential new:

У меня́ ещё боли́т плечо́ от э́той но́ши. (Литерату́рная газе́та, 14.6.67)	My shoulder still aches from this burden.

Apart from these general considerations, there are certain grammatical constructions where the frequency of the orders S—P and P—S differs from that stated above:

(i) If S is realised by a personal pronoun, it precedes P much more frequently—it occurs approximately 15 times as frequently as the order P—S. The usual order of a personal pronominal S preceding P is illustrated in the following example:

Она́ о́чень люби́ла Ива́на Ильича́, но ста́ла гнать его́ от себя́. (A. Tolstoy, Хожде́ние по му́кам)	She loved Ivan Il'ich very much but began to repulse him.

When the personal pronominal S follows P, it is contextually insignificant—it could be omitted from the clause without any loss of meaning. Note how, in the following example, the order of S and P changes from nominal S preceding P to personal pronominal S following P to the deletion of S altogether as the contextual significance of S diminishes:

Солда́ты привлека́ют Кре́йна свои́ми челове́ческими ка́чествами. Терпели́во перено́сят они́ лише́ния войны́, хо́лод и грязь око́пов. С дружелю́бием и ю́мором отно́сятся друг к дру́гу. (Изв АН СССР, сер лит и яз, vol. 24, 1965)	The soldiers attract Crane by their human qualities. They suffer patiently the deprivations of war, the cold and mud of the trenches. They treat each other with friendliness and humour.

In the following example the personal pronominal S is redundant because the form of the verb indicates the person who is performing the action:

Предви́жу я знако́мый вопро́с. (Литерату́рная газе́та, 22.11.66)	I foresee the familiar question.

Note that the personal pronominal S following P always follows immediately after P.

If the P is phased, the contextually insignificant personal pronominal S follows the first group in phase only, thus interrupting P:

Суме́л же он, не зна́я каза́хского языка́, переда́ть и глубоко́ национа́льный о́браз мышле́ния геро́ев и осо́бенности сти́ля своего́ дру́га. (Литерату́рная газе́та, 28.6.67)	He could, however, without knowing the Kazakh language, express both the deeply national way of thinking of the heroes and the peculiarities of the style of his friend.

The personal pronominal S very rarely stands at the end of a contextual unit. It may stand at the end of a clause provided that the following clause is part of the same contextual unit. Thus, in the following example, он is final in the clause but not in the contextual unit—the following beta conditioning time clause acts as essential new and the S as part of the non-essential new together with P:

Очну́лся он, когда́ со́лнце стоя́ло уже́ высоко́.
(Polevoy, По́весть о настоя́щем челове́ке)

He came to when the sun was already high in the sky.

On very rare occasions the personal pronominal S may be final in the clause and contextual unit acting as essential new. In such cases the essential new is extremely emphatic and is modified by an emphatic word:

Подо́бные же мучи́тельные колеба́ния испы́тываю и я.
(Литерату́рная газе́та, 14.6.67)

I, too, am experiencing such tormenting doubts.

(ii) If P introduces a beta reported clause, it usually immediately precedes the beta reported clause and thus follows S:

Тепе́рь он реши́л, что по́сле шко́лы пойдёт не в институ́т, а на заво́д.
(Chakovsky, Неве́ста)

Now he decided that after school he would not go to the institute but to the factory.

(iii) The order of S and P is fixed when introducing direct speech or thought. If S and P precede the direct speech or thought, S precedes P:

Она́ сказа́ла: «Зна́чит, тепе́рь же всё в поря́дке.»
(Granin, Иска́тели)

She said: 'So, now everything is in order.'

If S and P interrupt or follow the direct speech or thought, P precedes S:

«Расска́зы Ко́лосова, — писа́л А. Лунача́рский, — живы́е куски́ комсомо́льской жи́зни.»
(Изв АН СССР, сер лит и яз, vol. 24, 1965)

'Kolosov's stories', wrote A. Lunacharsky, 'are vivid slices of Komsomol life.'

— Това́рищ к вам с ра́портом, — сказа́л дежу́рный.
(A. Tolstoy, Хожде́ние по му́кам)

'A man to see you with a report,' said the guard.

(iv) In clauses containing only the elements S and P and, possibly, a linking, binding or parenthetic adjunct (A^1), the order P—S is more frequent, occurring about twice as often as the order S—P. This applies only to clauses forming a complete contextual unit by themselves, that is excluding those clauses where the essential new is realised by a following beta clause. Both orders are contextually determined. If P acts as non-essential new and S as essential new, P precedes S, as in the first clause of the following example:

Слы́шится му́зыка; [во мно́гих хи́жи-нах есть транзи́сторные приёмники.]
(Изве́стия, 31.11.66)

You can hear music: in many huts there are transistor radios.

The order P—S is very commonly found with verbs denoting the beginning, existence or concluding of a process:

Наступи́ло то вре́мя, когда́ фонари́ ещё не горе́ли, но могли́ вот-вот заже́чься.
(Paustovsky, Ска́зочник)

The time had come when the lamps were not yet burning, but could be lit at any moment.

Был небольшо́й моро́з, ти́хо, звёз-дно.
(Panova, Кружи́лиха)

There was a light frost, it was quiet, starry.

Прошло́ де́сять лет...
(Хи́мия и жизнь, 9.65)

Ten years have passed...

If S acts as given and P as new, S precedes P, as in the first two clauses in the following example:

В усло́виях, когда́ влия́ние пра́вящей демохристиа́нской па́ртии па́дает, а влия́ние коммуни́стов растёт, италья́н-ская буржуази́я принима́ет ме́ры к тому́, что́бы...
(Пра́вда, 4.11.66)

In conditions when the influence of the ruling Democratic Christian party is waning, while the influence of the Communists is growing, the Italian bourgeoisie takes steps to...

The order S—P is also found with verbs denoting the beginning, existence or concluding of a process, though here the new is more emphatic due to the overwhelming frequency of the reverse order. The order S—P is found in the second clause of the following example:

А́вторскому те́зису предстои́т по́л-ностью созре́ть лишь к фина́лу. А пока́ фина́л не наступи́л, нам сле́дует рассма́тривать встре́чи-галлюцина́ции не расшири́тельно а поу́же.
(Литерату́рная газе́та, 18.10.66)

The author's thesis should develop fully only towards the finale. And before the finale has begun, we should not examine the hallucinatory meetings expansively but a little more narrowly.

(v) If an A^2 precedes S and P and no element of clause structure follows the S and P, then provided that the clause is a complete contextual unit, i.e. provided that the essential new is not realised by a following beta clause, P precedes S approximately five times as frequently as the reverse order. The following example contains two clauses with the order A^2—P—S:

У костра́ сиде́ли дво́е — мужчи́на и же́нщина. В спи́ну им дул из степно́й ба́лки холо́дный ве́тер.
(A. Tolstoy, Хожде́ние по му́кам)

By the camp fire sat two people—a man and a woman. A cold wind blew on their backs from the steppe ravine.

This order is determined contextually: A^2 acts as given, P as non-essential new and S as essential new.

S may precede P, if it acts as given together with A^2, while P acts as new. This happens when S is pronominal:

Днём всё пря́чется... (Изве́стия, 31.11.66)	During the day everything hides...

This order is no more emphatic than the order A^2—P—S, exemplified above, since pronouns do not usually act as essential new and are thus not found usually at the end of a clause.

However, when S is realised by a noun in the order A^2—S—P, the new is often highly emphatic. One P may be contrasted with a following one:

С года́ми тво́рчество Кре́йна не развива́лось, а, наоборо́т, деградировало. (Изв АН СССР, сер лит и яз, vol. 24, 1965)	With the years Crane's work did not develop but, on the contrary, deteriorated.

P is frequently negative, as in the last clause of the following example:

Есть наро́дное изрече́ние: по́сле дра́ки кулака́ми не ма́шут. Но, во-пе́рвых, на на́шем писа́тельском съе́зде «дра́ки» не́ было. (Литерату́рная газе́та, 28.6.67)	There is a popular saying: don't wave your fists after a fight. But, in the first place, at our writers' congress there was no 'fight'.

P may, however, also be positive, especially if immediately preceding P is a second A^2 belonging to a class of A^2 which usually occupies this position in the clause (see subsection E):

В пути́ тра́ктор не́сколько раз остана́вливался. (Изве́стия, 31.11.66)	On the way the tractor stopped several times.

This last type of clause, in contrast to clauses with a negative P, is not highly emphatic.

If S and P preceded by an A^2 are followed by C or a second A^2, S precedes P fifteen times as often as the reverse order:

В э́тот же ве́чер Ма́слов показа́л Ка́те свои́ ру́кописи. (A. Tolstoy, Хожде́ние по му́кам)	On that same evening Maslov showed Katya his manuscripts.

P precedes S usually only if S is contextually insignificant. This happens (as has been shown above on p. 31) with a personal pronominal S:

Неред́ко переноси́лись они́ и в рабо́чие аудито́рии... (Изв АН СССР, сер лит и яз, vol. 24, 1965)	They were often carried over into the workers' groups...

as well as with a nominal S:

Так вот в отчёте «Литературной России» поставлен вопрос автору этих строк. (Литературная газета, 27.9.66)	And so in the report in *Literary Russia* the question is put to the author of these lines.

The order of S and P with a preceding C will be discussed in subsection C below on the order of the elements S, P and C.

в. *Predicator and complement*

P precedes C four times as frequently as C precedes P. When following P, C has one of three contextual roles. It may act as non-essential new when followed by another element of clause structure acting as essential new (A^2 in the following example):

Мальчик переделывал эти рассказы по-своему... (Paustovsky, Сказочник)	The boy adapted these stories in his own way...

or as essential new when final in the clause. The following sentence contains three examples:

Он опустил бинокль, вынул почернёвшую трубочку, не спеша насыпал в неё щепоть саратовской махорки. (A. Tolstoy, Хождение по мукам)	He put his binoculars down, took out a blackened pipe, unhurriedly filled it with a pinch of Saratov tobacco.

Thirdly, C may act as part of the new with no essential new and non-essential new distinguishable, as in the first clause of the following example:

Телегин явно невзлюбил её, обращался вежливо, но разговоров и встреч наедине избегал. (A. Tolstoy, Хождение по мукам)	Telegin clearly disliked her, behaved politely, but avoided conversations and meetings on their own.

The conditions in which this contextual analysis is found will be discussed in subsection C on the order of subject, predicator and complement.

If C precedes P, most frequently it acts as given, as in the last clause of the following example:

От духоты, от спирта, от мягкого света свечей сёстры казались очень хорошенькими...Одну звали Мушка. (A. Tolstoy, Хождение по мукам)	Because of the stuffiness, the alcohol, the soft light of the candles the sisters seemed very pretty...One of them was called Mushka.

It may also act as part of the new, in which no essential and non-essential new are distinguishable, as in the last clause of the following example:

3-2

...отрешённые от всего, что их окружа́ло...

(Chakovsky, Неве́ста)

...removed from everything that surrounded them...

In certain grammatical structures the frequency of the orders P—C and C—P differs from that quoted above:

(i) If P is realised by an infinitive, gerund or participle, C almost always follows P:

Христиа́н...уе́хал в столи́цу — Копенга́ген — завоёвывать сча́стье.

(Paustovsky, Ска́зочник)

Christian...left for the capital, Copenhagen, to seek his happiness.

Впереди́ идёт боево́е сохране́ние, при́данное на́шему отря́ду.

(Изве́стия, 31.11.66)

In front goes the military unit attached to our detachment.

C may precede P if it is realised by a pronoun—especially if it is a negative pronoun:

Под ним стоя́ла ничего́ не говори́вшая по́дпись: М. Шо́лох.

(Изв АН СССР, сер лит и яз, vol. 24, 1965)

Beneath it was the meaningless signature: M. Sholokh.

Тепе́рь, чтобы его́ доста́ть, на́до бы́ло поверну́ться на́ бок.

(Polevoy, По́весть о настоя́щем челове́ке)

Now, in order to get it, he had to turn over on his side.

C, when realised by a noun, may on rare occasions precede P:

Наро́д там быва́лый, скло́нный все жи́зненные явле́ния упроща́ть.

(Granin, Иска́тели)

The people there are experienced and tend to simplify all living phenomena.

With the exception of the negative pronominal C, the order C—P in such cases is a less usual stylistic variant of P—C.

(ii) In clauses containing the elements P and C and no S, in which P is realised by a third person plural verbal group, the order C—P is slightly more frequent than the order P—C. This construction is one method of translating the English passive into Russian. The order of the elements is determined by the contextual role of P and C. If C acts as given and P as part or the whole of the new, the order is C—P. The following example contains four clauses with the order C—P:

Двух челове́к расстреля́ли, а два́дцать молоды́х парне́й забра́ли и увели́ с собо́й. И мой сад...Все созре́вшие плоды́ обобра́ли, а дере́вья с недозре́вшими плода́ми вы́рубили.

(Изве́стия, 31.11.66)

Two men were shot and twenty young lads were taken and led away. And my garden...All the ripe fruit was pinched and the trees with unripe fruit were chopped down.

If P acts as given and C as part or the whole of the new, P precedes C:

36

Дважды обсуждали его поведение на партийном собрании.
(Правда, 13.11.66)

On two occasions his behaviour was discussed at a party meeting.

(iii) If the clause contains P and C^{E3} (see p. 15) in its structure, C^{E3} precedes P eight times as frequently as it follows. This is the complete opposite of the findings for the order of P and C in general. The order C—P is most frequently found with a personal pronominal C:

Тебе надо всё бросить и пойти служить дежурным монтёром...
(Granin, Искатели)

You must give up everything and go to work as a duty fitter...

but it is also found with a nominal C:

Для дальнейших попыток захватить Москву гитлеровскому командованию пришлось провести дополнительную подготовку.
(Известия, 5.12.66)

For its further attempts to capture Moscow the Hitler command had to make extra preparations.

If the personal pronominal C^{E3} follows P, it is contextually insignificant (cf. the personal pronominal S following P). The word тебе in the following example could be omitted without any change in meaning:

И вообще конфликт с конструктором кажется тебе чепухой.
(Granin, Искатели)

And in general the conflict with the constructor seems to you nonsensical.

One may also find a contextually insignificant nominal group following P:

...исследование тех условий, в которых приходилось жить и бороться советским людям в годы войны.
(Литературная газета, 6.10.66)

...investigation of the conditions in which the Soviet people had to live and struggle during the war years.

Occasionally the C^{E3} may follow P acting as essential new:

Они раскрывают изумительную целомудренную душу русской женщины лучше и полнее, чем, увы, это удаётся многим из нас пишущих.
(Литературная газета, 14.6.67)

They reveal the amazing chaste soul of the Russian woman better and more fully than, alas, many of us writers succeed in doing.

(iv) When the extensive complement (C^E) is realised by a personal pronoun, it precedes or follows P with approximately equal frequency. When following P, it always comes immediately after P, as in the last clause in the following example:

Трудно было бы ей жить с этим поэтом, если бы она не могла полюбить его...
(Paustovsky, Сказочник)

It would have been difficult for her to live with this poet, if she had not been able to fall in love with him...

and when preceding P, C usually comes immediately before it:

37

Повсю́ду Вас отлича́ла непоколеби́- мая ве́рность па́ртии и наро́ду. (Пра́вда, 20.12.66)	Everywhere you were distinguished by an unshakeable loyalty to the party and the people.

If it precedes P and is separated from it by another element of clause
structure, this element is usually an A^2 of the type which is usually found
immediately preceding P (see subsection E below):

Им обяза́тельно даю́тся парти́йные поруче́ния. (Пра́вда, 13.11.66)	They must be given party commissions.

Very occasionally, C is separated from P by S:

Тебе́ всегда́ э́то каза́лось абсолю́тно безразли́чным. (Granin, Иска́тели)	You always thought this a matter of complete indifference.

(v) If C^E is realised by a negative pronoun, it precedes P:

Весь свой путь от океа́на лосо́сь ничего́ не ест... (Изве́стия, 1.12.66)	For the whole of its journey from the ocean the salmon does not eat any- thing...

unless it is modified, in which case it follows P:

Но да́же и э́ти чу́ткие у́ши не слы́шали в лесу́ ничего́ кро́ме пти́чьей трес- котни́, сту́ка дя́тла и ро́вного зво́на сосно́вых верши́н. (Polevoy, По́весть о настоя́щем челове́ке)	But even these sensitive ears did not hear in the forest anything apart from the twittering of the birds, the tapping of the woodpecker and the steady ringing of the pine tops.

(vi) If C^E is realised by a reflexive pronoun, it almost always follows
P:

[С прихо́дом нача́льства маке́т немéд- ленно перестаёт рабо́тать.] Он ведёт себя́ так, как бу́дто он вообще́ никогда́ не рабо́тал. (Granin, Иска́тели)	With the arrival of the bosses the model immediately stops working. It behaves as if it had never worked at all.

It can on rare occasions precede P. This is a stylistic variant of P—C:

Ны́не тру́дно себе́ предста́вить од- ного́ поэ́та в ро́ли власти́теля дум. (Литерату́рная газе́та, 27.9.66)	Today it is difficult to imagine a single poet as a master of thoughts.

So far this subsection has been concerned with the order of clauses
containing one C and P. However, clauses often contain P and two Cs.
The most common classes of C occurring together in one clause are:
C^{E1} and C^{E2}, C^{E1} and C^{IC}.

(a) P, C^{E1}, C^{E2}

Most frequently both C^Es follow P. P and the first C^E act as non-
essential new and the second C^E as essential new. This applies whether
the order is P—C^{E1}—C^{E2}:

Он рабо́чий челове́к и презира́ет
лицеме́ров, кото́рые пою́т славо-
сло́вия рабо́чему кла́ссу...
(Chakovsky, Неве́ста)

He is a working man and despises
hypocrites, who sing the praises of the
working class...

or P—C^{E2}—C^{E1}:

...«жесто́кость и прожо́рливость»
предпринима́телей, кото́рые подвер-
га́ли нечелове́ческой эксплуата́ции
шахтёров...
(Изв АН СССР, сер лит и яз,
vol. 24, 1965)

...'the cruelty and greed' of the bosses,
who subjected the miners to inhuman
exploitation...

There are two grammatical factors which also influence the order.
First, if either C^E is pronominal, it will follow immediately after P.
Most frequently, C^{E2} is pronominal and is therefore found in the order
P—C^{E2}—C^{E1}, as in the last clause of the following example:

Де́ятельность э́тих офице́ров фло́та
нике́м не была́ «организо́вана», ни-
кто́ не дава́л им средств.
(Изве́стия, 1.12.66)

The activity of these naval officers was
not 'organised' by anyone, no one gave
them the means.

Occasionally, C^{E1} is pronominal and is found in the order P—C^{E1}—C^{E2},
as in the final clause of the following example:

Но е́сли ва́ше предприя́тие не про-
цвета́ет, бу́дьте че́стны и объясни́те
э́то ва́шим рабо́чим.
(Пра́вда, 7.12.66)

But if your undertaking is not flourishing,
be honest and explain this to your
workers.

Secondly, if P and C^E form a fixed expression, the C^E in the fixed
expression follows immediately after the P. Most frequently, the C^E in
such expressions is a C^{E1}. Common examples of fixed expressions are:

воздава́ть до́лжное	to give [somebody] his due
выража́ть благода́рность	to express gratitude
дава́ть объясне́ние	to give an explanation
ока́зывать по́мощь	to give help
отдава́ть предпочте́ние	to show a preference
подводи́ть ито́ги	to sum up
придава́ть значе́ние	to attach importance
придава́ть си́лы	to give strength
уделя́ть внима́ние	to pay attention

The order with such fixed expressions is, therefore, P—C^{E1}—C^{E2}:

Тя́га к зна́ниям, к но́вому, к Ле́нину,
кото́рый «хоть што» зна́ет, придаёт
си́лы Фо́мке в конфли́кте с отцо́м.
(Изв АН СССР, сер лит и яз,
vol. 24, 1965)

His gravitation to knowledge, to new
ideas, to Lenin, who at least knows
'something', gives Fomka strength in
his conflict with his father.

Наш наро́д, ве́рный интернациона́ль-
ному до́лгу, ока́зывал и впредь бу́дет
ока́зывать всесторо́ннюю по́мощь
герои́ческому вьетна́мскому наро́ду.
(Пра́вда, 31.12.66)

Our people, true to its international
duty, has given and will go on giving in
the future all-round help to the heroic
people of Vietnam.

P and C^{E2} can occasionally also form a fixed expression, resulting in the order P—C^{E2}—C^{E1}:

Мы нимало не склонны подвергать сомнению правомерность замечаний критиков о влиянии западной новеллы на раннего Паустовского.
(Изв АН СССР, сер лит и яз, vol. 24, 1965)

We are by no means inclined to doubt the fairness of the critics' remarks about the influence of the western short story on the early Paustovsky.

The next most frequent order has one C^E preceding P and the other one following. The contextual analysis here determines the order. One C^E acts as given, P and the other C^E act as non-essential and essential new respectively. The C^E acting as given precedes P, which in turn precedes the C^E acting as essential new. This results in both the order C^{E1}—P—C^{E2}:

Весь остаток моей жизни я посвящу неутомимому труду на благо нашей партии и советского народа...
(Правда, 20.12.66)

The whole of the rest of my life I will dedicate to tireless work for the good of our party and the Soviet people...

and the order C^{E2}—P—C^{E1}, as in the first clause of the following example:

Одним дают дельные советы, другим указывают на недостатки и помогают устранять их. (Правда, 13.11.66)

Some are given businesslike advice, others have their faults pointed out and are helped to avoid them.

On very rare occasions, both C^Es precede P. When they do so, one or both C^Es are pronominal. One of the C^Es may be a relative pronoun and thus initial in the clause:

...той ответственной работы, которую мне поручила партия.
(Правда, 20.12.66)

...the responsible work which the party has entrusted to me.

One of the C^Es may be realised by an unmodified negative pronoun, which precedes P:

Валя всё равно ничего ему не скажет.
(Chakovsky, Невеста)

All the same Valya won't tell him anything.

(b) P, C^{E1}, C^{IC}

In this structure C^{IC} almost always follows P and is usually found in the clause *after* C^{E1}. The orders most frequently found are: P—C^{E1}—C^{IC} and C^{E1}—P—C^{IC}. In the order P—C^{E1}—C^{IC}, P and C^{E1} act as non-essential new, and C^{IC} as essential new, as in the last clause of the following example:

Если бы я не знал, что у Ани есть сын — сын моего друга, я счёл бы нашу встречу галлюцинацией.
(Нева, No. 7, 1966)

If I had not known that Anya had a son—the son of my friend, I would have considered our meeting to be a hallucination.

In the order C^{E1}—P—C^{IC}, C^{E1} acts as given, P as non-essential new and C^{IC} as essential new:

Егó нельзя́ бы́ло назва́ть самовлю-
блённым и́ли самоуве́ренным.
(Chakovsky, Неве́ста)

You could not call him self-centred or
self-confident.

The order P—C^{IC}—C^{E1} is also found. Being less frequent (with C^{IC} preceding C^{E1}), it attracts greater emphasis:

Съезд признаёт чрезвыча́йно необхо-
ди́мым созда́ние литерату́ры для
рабо́че-крестья́нской молодёжи.
(Изв АН СССР, сер лит и яз,
vol. 24, 1965)

The congress recognises as extremely
necessary the creation of literature for
the worker-peasant youth.

Two factors influence the order of both Cs following P. First, if C^{E1} is pronominal, it precedes C^{IC}:

Ю́ноша А́ндерсен до́лго счита́л себя́
кем уго́дно — певцо́м, танцо́ром, де-
клама́тором, поэ́том, сати́риком и
драмату́ргом.
(Paustovsky, Ска́зочник)

The young Andersen for a long time
considered himself to be all sorts of
people—singer, dancer, declaimer, poet,
satirist and dramatist.

Secondly, if P and C^{IC} form a fixed expression, the order P—C^{IC}—C^{E1} is found:

па́ртии..., поста́вившей свое́й зада́чей
по́длинно национа́льное возрожде́ние
на ба́зе нау́чного социали́зма...
(Пра́вда, 7.12.66)

to the party...which has set as its task
a truly national regeneration based on
scientific socialism...

On very rare occasions, one further order is found: C^{IC}—P—C^{E1}. C^{IC} acts as given, P as non-essential new and C^{E1} as essential new:

Одно́й из свои́х гла́вных зада́ч
молодогварде́йцы счита́ли «студи́й-
ные собесе́дования.»
(Изв АН СССР, сер лит и яз,
vol. 24, 1965)

One of their main tasks the Young
Guards considered to be 'studio con-
versations'.

This is a very rare occurrence of C^{IC} preceding P.

If C^{IC} is realised by как plus a nominal group, it always follows both P and C^{E1}. Thus only two orders are possible, P—C^{E1}—C^{IC}:

Одна́ко, Ле́нин рассма́тривал тради́-
ции ста́рой культу́ры лишь как
исхо́дные для строи́тельства но́вой
культу́ры и иску́сства...
(Литерату́рная газе́та, 29.10.66)

However, Lenin considered the tradi-
tions of the old culture merely as a
starting point for the construction of a
new culture and art...

and C^{E1}—P—C^{IC}:

Спекта́кли де́ти почти́ всегда́ прини-
ма́ют как ска́зку.
(Paustovsky, Ска́зочник)

Children almost always consider the
theatre show to be a fairy tale.

c. *Subject, predicator and complement*

This subsection will be concerned with clauses containing S, P and one C—either C^{E1} or C^I. In each case two factors will be taken into consideration: the frequency of occurrence of a given order and the commonly occurring contextual functions of the elements in each order.

(*i*) S, P, C^{E1}

Most frequently the elements S, P and C^{E1} are found in the order S—P—C^{E1}. Next most frequent is the order C^{E1}—P—S, though even this is not very common. The remaining orders are found extremely rarely. The following table shows how frequently each order occurs considered as a percentage of the total occurrences of S, P and C^{E1} in any order:

S—P—C	79 %
S—C—P	1 %
P—S—C	1 %
P—C—S	2 %
C—S—P	4 %
C—P—S	11 %

Occurrences of one element interrupting another account for the remaining 2 %.

Each order will now be considered separately in descending order of frequency of occurrence.

(*a*) S—P—C^{E1}

The following contextual analyses are commonly found with this order of elements:

First, S acts as given, P as non-essential new and C as essential new, as in the final clause of the following example:

Делегáты от флóта съéхали нá берег и хмýро вы́слушали Вахрамéева, — он предлагáл самоуби́йство.
(А. Tolstoy, Хождéние по мýкам)

The delegates from the navy gathered on the shore and gloomily listened to Vakhrameyev—he was proposing suicide.

Secondly, S acts as given, P and C as new with no essential and non-essential new distinguishable. This happens in two types of clause—when C is realised by a personal pronoun:

Отвращéние к себé, к рабóте, к своéй рабóте переполня́ет тебя́...
(Granin, Искáтели)

Disgust with yourself, work, your own work fills you...

and when P and C are realised by a fixed expression, as in:

Однáко, подóбные попы́тки опорóчить искýсство социалисти́ческого реали́зма потерпéли крах.
(Литератýрная газéта, 29.10.66)

However, such attempts to tarnish the art of socialist realism were defeated.

42

Other such fixed expressions are:

вызыва́ть сожале́ние	to cause regret
де́лать вы́вод	to come to a conclusion
игра́ть роль	to play a part
име́ть значе́ние	to be of significance
име́ть пра́во	to have the right
име́ть смысл	to make sense
обраща́ть внима́ние	to pay attention
представля́ть интере́с	to be of interest
привлека́ть внима́ние	to attract attention
принима́ть уча́стие	to take part
производи́ть впечатле́ние	to make an impression

Thirdly, S acts as given, P and C as non-essential new and a following A^2 or beta clause as essential new:

Он посыла́л её за вино́м в сво́дчатый кирпи́чный по́греб.
   (A. Tolstoy, Хожде́ние по му́кам)

He used to send her for wine to the arched brick cellar.

Одна́ко, встре́ча с ю́ношей убеди́ла его́, что Ва́ля гото́ва соверши́ть неоправи́мую оши́бку.
   (Chakovsky, Неве́ста)

However, the meeting with the young man convinced him that Valya was prepared to commit an irrevocable error.

Fourthly, emphatic order of contextual elements is occasionally found. S acts as essential new, P and C as non-essential new:

И́менно дочь, мы́сли о ней, забо́ты о ней, любо́вь к ней должны́ бы́ли запо́лнить пустоту́, кото́рая образова́лась тепе́рь вокру́г Никола́я Константи́новича.

   (Chakovsky, Неве́ста)

It was his daughter, thoughts about her, worries about her, love for her, that must fill the emptiness which had formed now around Nikolay Konstantinovich.

(b) C^{E1}—P—S

The following contextual analyses are commonly found with this order of elements:

First, C acts as given, P as non-essential new and S as essential new:

Внима́ние его́ привлёк звук, послы́шавшийся све́рху.
   (Polevoy, По́весть о настоя́щем
            челове́ке)

His attention was attracted by a sound coming from above.

C is often pronominal:

Его́ высоко́ оце́нивали · и кри́тики после́дующих лет.
   (Изв АН СССР, сер лит и яз,
            vol. 24, 1965)

He was highly thought of even by critics of subsequent years.

Note that the English translation usually makes use of a passive construction.

Secondly, C acts as given, P and S as non-essential new and a following A^2 as essential new:

Удиви́тельные переме́ны принёс кол-
хо́зный строй и в быт куба́нских
казако́в.
(Литерату́рная газе́та, 28.6.67)

Remarkable changes were introduced by
the collective farming system even into
the life of the Kuban Cossacks.

This order is comparatively rare, the order C—S—P—A being more usual (see subsection *c* below).

Thirdly, the emphatic order of contextual elements is occasionally found. C acts as essential new, P and S as non-essential new:

К сожале́нию, и́менно тако́й хара́ктер
но́сит ны́нешнее объедине́ние социа́л-
демокра́тов и социали́стов в Ита́лии.
(Пра́вда, 4.11.66)

Unfortunately, it is just such a character
which the present union of Social-
Democrats and Socialists in Italy has.

(*c*) C^{E1}—S—P

The following contextual analyses are commonly found with this order of elements:

First, C and S act as given, P as non-essential new, a following A^2 or beta clause as essential new:

Э́тот пери́од свое́й жи́зни Крейн
описа́л зате́м в 1897 г. в автобиогра-
фи́ческом рома́не «Тре́тья фиа́лка».
(Изв АН СССР, сер лит и яз,
vol. 24, 1965)

This period of his life Crane described
later in 1897 in his autobiographical
novel *The Third Violet*.

Речь о ва́жности зака́за они́ слу́шают
чуть прищу́рясь.
(Granin, Иска́тели)

The speech about the importance of the
order they listen to with their eyes
slightly narrowed.

C and S are often pronominal:

Э́то я по́нял гора́здо по́зже.
(Paustovsky, Ска́зочник)

I understood this much later.

Secondly, C and S act as given, P and a following A^2 as new, no essential or non-essential new is distinguishable because A^2 is pronominal:

[И вме́сте с тем — здесь красота́ не
про́сто за́мкнутый мир...,] кото́рый
ка́ждый избра́нник несёт в себе́...
(Изв АН СССР, сер лит и яз,
vol. 24, 1965)

And furthermore—here beauty is not
simply the closed world...which every
chosen man bears within himself...

or P and A^2 are realised by a fixed expression such as вы́разить слова́ми:

...и мно́гое друго́е, чего́ Кудря́вцев
не мог бы вы́разить слова́ми.
(Chakovsky, Неве́ста)

...and much else which Kudryavtsev
could not put into words.

44

Thirdly, C and S act as given, P as new. S is usually pronominal and P usually negative; the clause stresses that something was not achieved:

Однако, адеква́тного худо́жественного эффе́кта мы не получа́ем...
(Изв АН СССР, сер лит и яз, vol. 24, 1965)

However, we do not get an adequate artistic effect...

Fourthly, emphatic order of contextual elements is occasionally found. C acts as essential new, S and P as non-essential new:

Из свои́х 24 лет шесть он провёл в а́рмии.
(Изве́стия, 31.11.66)

Of his 24 years six were spent in the army.

This clause stresses that he had been in the army for as long as six years.

(*d*) P—C^{E1}—S

The following contextual analyses are commonly found with this order of elements:

First, P and C act as non-essential new, S as essential new. This is found with a contextually insignificant pronominal C, which in this structure tends to follow rather than precede P:

Создаёт её в коне́чном счёте большо́й коллекти́в одарённых люде́й.
(Литерату́рная газе́та, 28.6.67)

In the final result it is created by a large group of gifted men.

Compare the order C^{E1}—P—S with a contextually significant pronominal C^{E1} (see subsection *b* above). This order is also found with a contextually insignificant C^{E1} realised by a proper name:

Бо́льше всего́ порази́ло Кудря́вцева то, что никто́ из делега́тов конфе́ренции не предложи́л включи́ть его́ кандидату́ру дополни́тельно.
(Chakovsky, Неве́ста)

Most of all Kudryavtsev was struck by the fact that none of the delegates of the conference had proposed the supplementary inclusion of his candidature.

Secondly, P and C act as given, S as new. P and C are realised by a fixed expression such as those listed in subsection *a* above:

Привлека́ют внима́ние два сатири́ческих отры́вка.
(Изв АН СССР, сер лит и яз, vol. 24, 1965)

Two satirical passages attract attention.

Note that P and C realised by a fixed expression are found following S when acting as new:

И всё-таки э́то не име́ет принципиа́льного значе́ния.
(Изв АН СССР, сер лит и яз, vol. 24, 1965)

And all the same this is not of great significance.

When acting as given, P and C realised by a fixed expression precede S in the order P—C—S as is illustrated in the example before last. If, however, C is modified, it will precede P in the more usual order C—P—S:

Огро́мную роль в мобилиза́ции наро́дных сил сыгра́ла Моско́вская парти́йная организа́ция. (Изве́стия, 5.12.66)	The Moscow party organisation played a most important part in the mobilisation of the nation's forces.

Here the fixed expression is broken; C acts as given, P as non-essential new and S as essential new.

(*e*) S—C^{E1}—P

The following contextual analyses are commonly found with this order of elements:

First, S acts as given, C and P as new with no essential and non-essential new distinguishable. A following pronominal A^2 sometimes acts as new together with C and P. C is always pronominal. The following passage contains one example of C realised by a negative pronoun and one by a demonstrative pronoun:

Не говори́те им, как сейча́с мно́гие э́то де́лают: «Ва́ше прави́тельство ничего́ не хо́чет сде́лать для нас.» (Пра́вда, 7.12.66)	Don't tell them, as many do nowadays: 'Your government does not want to do anything for us.'

Secondly, S acts as given, C and P as non-essential new and a following A^2 or beta clause as essential new. C is pronominal:

На́ша нау́ка мно́гое сде́лала для того́, что́бы удовлетворя́ть э́тот спрос. (Изве́стия, 11.11.66)	Our science has done a lot to satisfy this demand.

Thirdly, S acts as given, C as non-essential new and P as essential new. P is usually negative. This order is highly emphatic:

Комбина́ция из углеро́да и водоро́да бо́льшего дать не мо́жет. (Хи́мия и жизнь, 6.65)	A combination of carbon and hydrogen cannot give any more.

Fourthly, in the spoken language and in imitations of it in literature emphatic order of contextual elements is found. S acts as given, C as essential new and P as non-essential new, as in the last clause of the following example:

Éсли бы Ва́ля влюби́лась в хоро́шего, де́льного ю́ношу, — ду́мал Кудря́вцев, — что ж, я всё сде́лал бы для сча́стья до́чери… (Chakovsky, Неве́ста)	'If Valya had fallen in love with a good serious young man', thought Kudryavtsev, 'well, I would have done everything for my daughter's happiness…

Being a fairly common structure in the spoken language, it attracts less emphasis than other examples of the emphatic order of contextual elements.

(f) P—S—C^{E1}

The following contextual analyses are commonly found with this order of elements:

First, P and S act as non-essential new, C as essential new. S is realised either by a contextually insignificant personal pronoun, as in the final clause of the following example:

...пе́рвые ещё неуве́ренные уда́ры проснувшегося дя́тла, раздава́вшиеся в тишине́ ле́са так музыка́льно, бу́дто долби́л он не древе́сный ствол, а по́лое те́ло скри́пки...
(Polevoy, По́весть о настоя́щем челове́ке)

...the first as yet unsure blows of the awakened woodpecker which resounded in the quiet of the forest just as musically as if he had been pecking away not at a tree trunk but at the hollow body of a violin...

or by a contextually insignificant nominal group. This may be a proper noun:

Так обознача́ет Н. Шамота́ гла́вное направле́ние своего́ эстети́ческого ана́лиза...
(Литерату́рная газе́та, 3.12.66)

This is how N. Shamota indicates the main direction of his aesthetic analysis...

but need not necessarily be so:

С до́брым све́тлым чу́вством провожа́ют сове́тские лю́ди год 1966.
(Пра́вда, 31.12.66)

With a fine joyous feeling the Soviet people bid farewell to the year 1966.

Secondly, this order is found in alpha and beta reported question clauses introduced by the interrogative adjunct ли. P is most frequently initial and is followed by S and C in that order, as in the first clause of the following example:

Начнёт ли батальо́н Сабу́рова марш к Сталингра́ду, не дожида́ясь остальны́х батальо́нов, и́ли же, по́сле ночёвки, у́тром сра́зу дви́нется весь полк...
(Simonov, Дни и но́чи)

Will Saburov's battalion start its march to Stalingrad without waiting for the remaining battalions, or, on the other hand, will the whole regiment set off all together in the morning, after a night's rest...

Table 2 below summarises the contextual role of each element in each order.

Note that on only two occasions do two orders of elements have the same contextual analysis. The second and third analyses of S—P—C are identical respectively with the first two of the order S—C—P. The order S—C—P is always found when C is realised by a negative pronominal group, provided that it is not modified (see p. 38), and is sometimes found when C is realised by another class of pronominal group. In this latter case the orders S—P—C and S—C—P are stylistic variants.

TABLE 2

	S	P	C	(A² or beta clause)
S—P—C	G	NEN	EN	
	G	N	N	
	G	NEN	NEN	EN
emphatic	EN	NEN	NEN	
C—P—S	EN	NEN	G	
	NEN	NEN	G	EN
emphatic	NEN	NEN	EN	
C—S—P	G	NEN	G	EN
	G	N	G	N
	G	N	G	
emphatic	NEN	NEN	EN	
P—C—S	EN	NEN	NEN	
	N	G	G	
S—C—P	G	N	N	(N)
	G	NEN	NEN	EN
	G	EN	NEN	
emphatic	G	NEN	EN	
P—S—C	NEN	NEN	EN	
		Question clauses with ли		

G—Given; NEN—Non-essential new; EN—Essential new; N—New (no essential or non-essential new distinguishable).

It is significant that P rarely acts as essential new, or as new on its own. On the two occasions this occurs (in the orders C—S—P and S—C—P) the orders are highly emphatic. P is also never found acting as essential new in clauses with an emphatic order of contextual elements. It must be stressed that the contextual analyses examined are ones that are found frequently in written Russian and do not cover all the potentially possible ones.

The highly emphatic orders of S, P and C are those which either have an emphatic order of contextual elements (the essential new preceding the non-essential new) or have rarely occurring orders of S, P and C where these orders are determined solely on the basis of given and new. However, when the order of S, P and C has been brought about by such factors as contextually insignificant personal pronominal groups, fixed expressions, negative pronominal groups or the presence of the interrogative adjunct ли, the resultant order, however rarely it may occur, is not especially emphatic.

There are occasions when the grammatical inflexions do not distinguish S from C^{E1}. This happens when the nominative and accusative cases of both the noun realising S and the noun realising C^{E1} are identical in form. The nouns must also be of the same number and, if the verb is past tense singular, of the same gender; otherwise the verbal ending will distinguish which noun is realising S and which C^{E1}. Thus in the frequently quoted example мать любит дочь the function of the two nominal groups in the clause is potentially ambiguous. The clause could mean either 'the mother loves her daughter' or 'the daughter loves her mother'—in other words, this clause has the elements S, P, C^{E1} in either the order S—P—C^{E1} or the order C^{E1}—P—S. The first analysis (S—P—C^{E1}) is more likely, because of the overwhelming frequency of this order. However, it is not the only possible one. The order of elements does not determine their function. Though the function of the nominal groups may be ambiguous in an isolated clause, in context the function of the nominal groups is almost always clear. When S and C^{E1} cannot be distinguished by the inflexions, the order S—P—C^{E1} is slightly more frequent than when S and C^{E1} can be distinguished by the inflexions.

Thus most frequently the order S—P—C is found, as in:

В районе г. Калинина наши войска отбили попытки врага развить наступление. (Известия, 5.12.66)

In the region of Kalinin our armies repulsed attempts by the enemy to develop an attack.

События последнего десятилетия захватывают все стороны нашего существования.
(Литературная газета, 6.10.66)

The events of the last decade embrace all sides of our existence.

However, other orders are also found—P—C—S:

Вызывает сожаление только тот факт, что в этот сборник не вошли многие рассказы, являющиеся особенно характерными для Крейна...
(Изв АН СССР, сер лит и яз,
vol. 24, 1965)

The only fact one regrets is that this collection did not include many of the stories which are especially characteristic of Crane...

C—P—S:

Каждый такой объект бомбит звено реактивных бомбардировщиков.
(Известия, 31.11.66)

Every such object is bombed by a squadron of jet fighters.

(ii) S, P, C^I

As with S, P, C^{E1} the order S—P—C is the most frequent and C—P—S next most frequent. S—P—C is found in 72% of the total occurrences of structures with S, P, C^I (a lower percentage than for S—P—C^{E1}) and C—P—S on 23% (a considerably higher percentage than for C^{E1}—P—S). Of the remaining orders only P—C—S occurs at all frequently—in 4% of the total occurrences of S, P, C^I.

The order of elements is influenced by the following two factors. First, the frequency of occurrence in certain orders varies according to the class of group realising C^I. If C^I is realised by a nominal group in the nominative case, the order is almost always S—P—C:

Три че́тверти рабо́тающих на строи́тельстве оборони́тельных рубеже́й бы́ли же́нщины.
(Изве́стия, 5.12.66)

Three-quarters of those working on the construction of the defences were women.

If C^I is realised by a short adjectival group, S—P—C is still the most frequent order:

По пла́ну она́ [фа́брика] должна́ быть гото́ва в четвёртом кварта́ле ны́нешнего го́да.
(Изве́стия, 24.11.66)

According to the plan it [the factory] should be ready in the fourth quarter of the present year.

C—P—S and P—C—S are found equally as frequently as each other, when C^I is realised by a short adjective—each order is found in 18 % of the total occurrences:

Столь же сло́жен был проце́сс духо́вного перело́ма, приня́тия но́вой револю́цио́нной действи́тельности у таки́х писа́телей как Э. Багри́цкий, И. Ба́бель.
(Изв АН СССР, сер лит и яз, vol. 24, 1965)

Just as complex was the process of spiritual crisis, of the acceptance of the new revolutionary reality, with such writers as E. Bagritsky, I. Babel'.

Шля́пу он нёс в руке́, и потому́ был хорошо́ ви́ден его́ большо́й пока́тый лоб.
(Paustovsky, Ска́зочник)

He carried his cap in his hand and therefore you could see quite clearly his big sloping forehead.

The difference in the contextual roles of S, P and C in the orders S—P—C, C—P—S and P—C—S is discussed below (pp. 51–2).

Secondly, the verbal group realising P influences the order of the elements. If P is realised by служи́ть or явля́ться the order C—P—S is slightly more frequent than the order S—P—C (which otherwise is the most frequent order). The following two examples illustrate the use of явля́ться in the most frequent order C—P—S and in the slightly less frequent order S—P—C:

Гла́венствующим при́нципом объедине́ния двух па́ртий явля́ется углубле́ние раско́ла рабо́чего движе́ния.
(Пра́вда, 4.11.66)

The dominant principle in the union of the two parties is the deepening of the split in the workers' movement.

И э́то воспита́ние явля́ется обя́занностью всех без исключе́ния руководи́телей.
(Изве́стия, 24.11.66)

And this education is the duty of all our leaders without exception.

The following two examples illustrate the use of служи́ть in the orders
C—P—S and S—P—C, respectively:

Исхо́дным моме́нтом для созда́ния но́вой, социалисти́ческой культу́ры мо́гут послужи́ть лу́чшие достиже́ния и́менно ста́рого иску́сства.
(Литерату́рная газе́та, 29.10.66)

The best achievements of just this old art can serve as the starting point for the creation of a new socialist culture.

Коммунисти́ческая парти́йность его́ тво́рчества...слу́жит осно́вой свобо́дного сотру́дничества социалисти́ческого иску́сства с наро́дом.
(Литерату́рная газе́та, 3 12.66)

The communist party nature of his writing...serves as the basis for the free cooperation of socialist art with the people.

The difference in the contextual roles of S, P and C in the orders S—P—C and C—P—S is discussed in subsections *a* and *b* below.

Each of the commonly occurring orders of S, P, C^I will now be examined:

(*a*) S—P—C^I

The following contextual analyses are commonly found with this order of elements:

First, S acts as given, P as non-essential new, C as essential new:

Те в А́фрике, кто хо́чет стро́ить социали́зм, стано́вятся для империали́зма враго́м но́мер оди́н.
(Пра́вда, 7.12.66)

Those in Africa who want to build socialism are becoming for imperialism enemy number one.

Что́ они́ бомбя́т, остаётся зага́дкой.
(Изве́стия, 31.11.66)

What they are bombing is still a mystery.

Secondly, S acts as given, P and C as non-essential new and a following A^2 as essential new:

Молоды́е писа́тели «Комсомо́лии» бы́ли бли́зки Шо́лохову и темати́чески и по свои́м иде́йным тво́рческим пози́циям.
(Изв АН СССР, сер лит и яз, vol. 24, 1965)

The young writers of the *Komsomoliya* were close to Sholokhov both thematically and in their ideological creative positions.

(*b*) C^I—P—S

C and P act as given, S as new:

И привы́чными стано́вятся ссы́лки на отстава́ние кри́тики от жи́зни.
(Литерату́рная газе́та, 3.12.66)

References to the critics' isolation from life are becoming usual.

В после́днее вре́мя бо́льше ста́ло собра́ний с интере́сными пове́стками дня.
(Пра́вда, 13.11.66)

Recently meetings with interesting agendas have grown more common.

4-2

(c) P—C^I—S

P and C act as given, S as new (in the second example S is realised by a rank-shifted clause):

Сра́зу ста́ли слы́шны все преду́тренние лесны́е зву́ки.
   (Polevoy, По́весть о настоя́щем человѐке)

Straightaway one could hear all the dawn forest sounds.

Ста́нет поня́тно, почему́ столь ва́жно нара́щивать мо́щность генера́торов.
   (Изве́стия, 11.11.66)

It will become clear why it is so important to increase the power of the generators.

It will be noted that the contextual analysis of the orders C—P—S and P—C—S is identical. In certain structures the order P—C—S is obligatory. When P is realised by the word не, the negative form of the present tense of the verb быть, it will always precede C:

Не я́сно, как и в каку́ю сто́рону потя́нется цепо́чка после́дствий стихи́йного бойко́та.
   (Литерату́рная газе́та, 18.10.66)

It is not clear how and in what direction the chain of consequences of the elemental boycott will move.

If P and C are realised by a fixed expression such as ста́ли не ре́дкостью, бы́ло бы оши́бкой the order will be P—C—S:

Ста́ли не ре́дкостью загла́вия рома́нов «Честь», «Со́весть» и т. п.
   (Литерату́рная газе́та, 6.10.66)

Such titles of novels as *Honour, Conscience,* etc. are no longer a rarity.

Otherwise, the two orders are stylistic variants. The order C—P—S is more frequent, unless C is realised by a short adjective in which case both orders are equally frequent.

(d) P—S—C^I

This order is found in alpha and beta question clauses with the interrogative adjunct ли:

Был ли Кудря́вцев плохи́м челове́ком?
   (Chakovsky, Невѐста)

Was Kudryavtsev a bad man?

D. *Subject and intensive complement*

In clauses containing a subject and intensive complement but no predicator the order of the elements depends both on the contextual role of each element and on the class of group realising C^I. Each class of group commonly found realising C^I will now be examined in detail taking account of the contextual role of each order of elements.

(i) Short adjective

If C^I is realised by a short adjectival group, it follows S slightly more frequently than it precedes. The class of group realising S must also be taken into account. S may be realised, on the one hand, by a nominal or pronominal group and, on the other, by a rank-shifted clause.

If S is realised by a (pro-)nominal group, the order S—C is twice as frequent as the reverse order:

Банкро́тство коммуни́зма очеви́дно.
(Пра́вда, 4.11.66)

The bankruptcy of communism is evident.

[Мы ча́ще говори́м о перево́дах на ру́сский язы́к.] И э́то закономе́рно.
(Литерату́рная газе́та, 28.6.67)

Most frequently we talk of translations into Russian. And this is fair enough.

Both of these examples have S acting as given and C^I as new. Occasionally, S may act as given and C^I as non-essential new; a following A^2 or beta clause acts as essential new:

В лаборато́рии всё гото́во к приёму долгожда́нного го́стя.
(Granin, Иска́тели)

In the laboratory everything is ready to receive the long-awaited guest.

Поэ́тому, все мы, Ва́ши друзья́ и това́рищи, о́чень ра́ды, что в день шестидесятиле́тия Вы удосто́ены вы́сшей награ́ды Сове́тского Сою́за.
(Пра́вда, 20.12.66)

Therefore, all of us, your friends and comrades, are very glad that on your sixtieth birthday you have been honoured with the highest award of the Soviet Union.

More rarely, emphatic order of contextual elements is found. S acts as essential new, C^I as non-essential new. S is usually modified by an emphatic word:

В «Сора́нге» далеко́ не всё безупре́чно.
(Изв АН СССР, сер лит и яз, vol. 24, 1965)

In *Sorang* by no means everything is beyond reproach.

In the order C—S most frequently C^I acts as given, S as new:

Весьма́ актуа́льна для на́шей эсте́тики сего́дня глубо́кая, по́длинно нау́чная разрабо́тка пробле́м реалисти́ческого худо́жественного воспроизведе́ния действи́тельности в социалисти́ческом о́бществе.
(Литерату́рная газе́та, 29.10.66)

Very important for our aesthetics today is a deep, genuinely scientific development of the problems of realistic literary reproduction of actuality in a socialist society.

Occasionally, C^I and S may act as non-essential new and a following A^2 or beta clause as essential new. This analysis is rare and is only found when S is realised by a contextually insignificant group (usually pronominal):

Знаменáтельно онó, потому́ что... | It is important because...Paustovsky
Паустóвский продолжáл увлекáться | continued to be carried away by the world
ми́ром фантáзии, гри́новским ми́ром | of fantasy, by Green's world of 'the real
«реáльного в нереáльном». | in the unreal'.
(Изв АН СССР, сер лит и яз, vol. 24, 1965)

If S is realised by a rank-shifted clause, it almost always follows C^I. C^I acts as given and S as new:

Бесполéзно обращáться к тебé в э́ти | It is useless to come to you during this
дни с каки́ми-нибудь делáми. | period on business.
(Granin, Искáтели)

Характéрно, что в рассказе Шóлохов | It is characteristic that in the story
перенёс дéйствие в знакóмую ему́ | Sholokhov transferred the action to the
казáчью срéду. | Cossack environment which he knew.
(Изв АН СССР, сер лит и яз, vol. 24, 1965)

Широкó извéстно, как акти́вно выступáл | It is well known how actively Vladimir
Влади́мир Ильи́ч прóтив пролет- | Il'ich fought against the members of the
кýльтовских ниспроверга́телей стáрого | Proletkult who rejected the old cultural
культýрного наслéдия. | inheritance.
(Литератýрная газéта, 29.10.66)

Very occasionally, S precedes C^I with S acting as given and C^I as new. The new here is emphasised by virtue of the rarity of occurrence of this order:

В повествовáтельном жáнре вóвсе | In the narrative genre to get completely
уйти́ от конкрéтности нелегкó. | away from concrete reality is not easy.
(Литератýрная газéта, 18.10.66)

A third order of S and C^I is also found. C^I may interrupt S. This occurs when an element from the rank-shifted clause precedes C^I in the main clause. In the following example an A^2 from the rank-shifted clause (в слóжной биогрáфии Áндерсена) precedes C^I (нелегкó) which, in turn, precedes the remainder of the rank-shifted clause (установи́ть то врéмя, когдá...). The A^2 at the beginning of the clause acts as given, C^I as non-essential new and the second part of the rank-shifted clause (from установи́ть to the end of the clause) as essential new:

В слóжной биогрáфии Áндерсена | In the complex biography of Andersen
нелегкó установи́ть то врéмя, когдá | it is not easy to establish the time when
он нáчал писáть свои́ пéрвые чудéсные | he started writing his first magic fairy
скáзки. | tales.
(Paustovsky, Скáзочник)

(ii) Comparative adjective

C^I, when realised by a comparative adjectival group, follows S slightly more frequently than it precedes. As with the short adjectival group, the order of S and C^I differs according to whether S is realised by a (pro-)nominal group or a rank-shifted clause.

When S is realised by a (pro-)nominal group, it usually precedes C^I. S acts as given, C^I as new:

Интере́сы бу́дущего предпочти́тель-нее интере́сов сего́дняшнего дня. (Chakovsky, Неве́ста)

The interests of the future are preferable to those of the present day.

When S is realised by a rank-shifted clause, C^I almost always precedes S. C^I acts as given, S as new:

[Непра́вильно называ́ть э́то сво́йство уме́нием.] Гора́здо верне́е назва́ть его́ тала́нтом. (Paustovsky, Ска́зочник)

It is incorrect to call this quality an ability. It is much more accurate to call it a talent.

Very occasionally, S precedes C^I with S acting as given and C^I as new. The new here is emphasised by virtue of its rarity of occurrence in this position:

Но вы́делить руби́дий значи́тельно сложне́е чем о́лово и́ли свине́ц. (Хи́мия и жизнь, 12.65)

But to isolate rubidium is much more complicated than tin or lead.

The rank-shifted clause realising S may also be interrupted by C^I. In the following example э́тот мета́лл acts as given, ле́гче as non-essential new and обраба́тывать as essential new:

Э́тот мета́лл ле́гче обраба́тывать.

This metal is easier to work.

(Cf. the structure with C^I realised by a short adjectival group, p. 54.)

(iii) Nominal group in the nominative case

If C^I is realised by a nominal group in the nominative case, it almost always follows S. S acts as given and C^I as new:

Никола́й Никола́евич — пе́рвый секрета́рь горко́ма. (Изве́стия, 1.12.66)

Nikolay Nikolayevich is the first secretary of the town committee.

Emphatic order of contextual elements is also found. S acts as essential new preceding C^I acting as non-essential new. An emphatic word usually modifies S. This is illustrated in the final clause of the following example:

Нам нет нужды́ боя́ться пока́зывать свои́ достиже́ния и побе́ды, потому́ что и́менно они́ — суть са́мой приро́ды сове́тского стро́я. (Литерату́рная газе́та, 28.6.67)

We have no need to fear showing our achievements and victories, because it is they which are the essence of the very nature of the Soviet system.

The order S—C is so widespread because the function of the elements S and C^I in the clause, when both are realised by nominal groups in the nominative case, is determined by their position relative to each other. If the first example of this subsection were to have the two nominal groups in the reverse order, the order of the elements (S—C) would remain the same, but the function of both groups would be changed:

Пе́рвый секрета́рь горко́ма — Никола́й Никола́евич.	The first secretary of the town committee is Nikolay Nikolayevich.

Very occasionally, another order of the elements S and C^I realised by a nominal group in the nominative case is found. C^I may be interrupted by S. The first part of the C^I acts as given together with S, the second part as new:

Литера́тор я уже́ немолодо́й. (Литерату́рная газе́та, 14.6.67)	I am no longer a young writer.

A similar construction is discussed in section 3 (see p. 76).

(iv) Rank-shifted clause

If C^I is realised by a rank-shifted clause, S precedes C^I. S acts as given, C^I as new. S is realised either by such nouns as цель, зада́ча, долг:

Их цель — иссле́довать и возврати́ть свое́й стране́ богате́йший край... (Изве́стия, 1.12.66)	Their aim is to explore and return to their country a very rich area...

or, alternatively, by the pronoun э́то in apposition to another, preceding rank-shifted clause:

Но чего́ я никогда́ не разреша́л себе́ — так э́то обма́нывать чита́теля полупра́вдой. (Литерату́рная газе́та, 14.6.67)	But what I never allowed myself to do was to deceive the reader with half-truths.

E. *The position of A^2 in the clause*

The position of A^2 in the clause varies according to its contextual role and according to the class of A^2. Further variation is noted within each class of A^2 depending on the class of group realising the A^2. An A^2 may be realised by one of three classes of group: adverbial; preposition-plus-complement; nominal. The nominal group may be in one of three cases—accusative, genitive, instrumental. Each of the classes of A^2 is not necessarily realised by all of these three classes of group. Thus, for example, adjuncts of time can be realised by each of these three classes, while adjuncts of cause are never realised by a nominal group.

A^2 has one of three contextual roles in the clause and for each role it occupies a particular position in the clause. The A^2 acting as given (постепе́нно and в на́шем уе́зде in the following two examples) stands at the beginning of the clause:

Постепе́нно Никола́й Константи́нович пристрасти́лся к реше́нию ша́хматных зада́ч. (Chakovsky, Неве́ста)	Gradually Nikolay Konstantinovich developed a passion for solving chess problems.
В на́шем уе́зде по́сле освобожде́ния была́ проведена́ земе́льная рефо́рма. (Изве́стия, 31.11.66)	In our district after liberation land reform was carried out.

When acting as non-essential new, A^2 may stand immediately before P (as постепе́нно) or immediately after P (as в на́шем уе́зде):

Никола́й Константи́нович постепе́нно пристрасти́лся к реше́нию ша́хматных зада́ч.	Nikolay Konstantinovich gradually developed a passion for solving chess problems.
По́сле освобожде́ния была́ проведена́ в на́шем уе́зде земе́льная рефо́рма.	After liberation in our district land reform was carried out.

In general, A^2s realised by an adverbial group precede P when acting as non-essential new and those realised by a preposition-plus-complement group follow.

When acting as essential new, A^2 stands at the end of the clause:

Никола́й Константи́нович пристрасти́лся к реше́нию ша́хматных зада́ч постепе́нно.	Nikolay Konstantinovich developed a passion for solving chess problems gradually.
По́сле освобожде́ния земе́льная рефо́рма была́ проведена́ в на́шем уе́зде.	After liberation land reform was carried out in our district.

For greater emphasis an emphatic word may be inserted before the A^2:

Никола́й Константи́нович пристрасти́лся к реше́нию ша́хматных зада́ч то́лько постепе́нно.	Nikolay Konstantinovich developed a passion for solving chess problems only gradually.
По́сле освобожде́ния земе́льная рефо́рма была́ проведена́ и в на́шем уе́зде.	After liberation land reform was carried out in our district too.

For even greater emphasis the A^2 may be placed at the beginning of the clause as well as being modified by an emphatic word. This results in an emphatic order of contextual elements (essential new preceding non-essential new):

То́лько постепе́нно Никола́й Константи́нович пристрасти́лся к реше́нию ша́хматных зада́ч.	Only gradually did Nikolay Konstantinovich develop a passion for solving chess problems.
И в на́шем уе́зде по́сле освобожде́ния была́ проведена́ земе́льная рефо́рма.	Even in our district land reform was carried out after liberation.

Although, as has just been shown, A^2 may act as given, non-essential or essential new, each class of A^2 and each class of group realising A^2 has its preferred contextual role in the clause and will therefore be found most frequently in one particular position. For example, an A^2 realised by an adverbial group tends to act as non-essential new. When acting as essential new, it bears more emphasis even without the presence of an emphatic modifier.

Each class of A^2 will now be discussed and within each class of A^2 the groups which commonly realise the particular class will be treated separately.

(i) Time

(a) Adverbial group

The adjunct of time realised by an adverbial group (adverbial adjunct of time) most frequently acts as non-essential new immediately preceding P:

Проблéма врéмени всегдá заводи́ла в тупи́к человéческий рáзум. (Изв АН СССР, сер лит и яз, vol. 24, 1965)	The problem of time has always baffled the human mind.
Мы дóлго бесéдовали. (Извéстия, 31.11.66)	We had a long talk.

Slightly more than half of all occurrences are found in this position.

The adverbial adjuncts of time ещё and ужé are almost always found immediately preceding P:

У негó ужé был свой сóбственный домáшний кýкольный теáтр. (Paustovsky, Скáзочник)	He already had his own home puppet theatre.
Звёзды ещё сверкáли óстро и хóлодно. (Polevoy, Пóвесть о настоя́щем человéке)	The stars were still shining sharply and coldly.

So strong is this tendency for ещё and ужé to be found immediately preceding P, that they also precede gerunds and participles, especially when they are negative:

Крейн написáл «Áлый знак дóблести», ещё не поню́хав пóроха. (Изв АН СССР, сер лит и яз, vol. 24, 1965)	Crane wrote *The Red Badge of Courage*, having as yet not smelt gunpowder.
...рáны, ещё не зажи́вшие до концá. (Chakovsky, Невéста)	...wounds which had not yet completely healed.

Other adverbial adjuncts of time tend to follow participles and gerunds (see below, p. 59).

The negative adverbial adjunct of time никогдá, in common with other negative adverbial adjuncts and complements, is always found before P:

Эти «па́ртии» никогда́ не по́льзо- | These 'parties' never enjoyed the support
вались подде́ржкой масс. | of the masses.
(Пра́вда, 7.12.66)

An adverbial adjunct of time may also act as non-essential new immediately following P, provided that it is not the final element in the clause:

«Се́верная по́весть» печа́талась впер- | *The Northern Tale* was printed in the
вы́е как три отде́льных расска́за. | first place as three separate stories.
(Изв АН СССР, сер лит и яз,
vol. 24, 1965)

Here the adverbial adjunct of time acquires greater emphasis than when it precedes P. However, when P is realised by a participle or a gerund, the adverbial adjunct of time usually follows P:

...в програ́мме, опира́вшейся тепе́рь | ...in the programme, now based on a
на реа́льную жи́зненную осно́ву... | real true-to-life foundation...
(Изв АН СССР, сер лит и яз,
vol. 24, 1965)

Here there is no special emphasis on the adjunct. Note, however, that ещё and уже́ precede the gerund and participle (see above, p. 58).

The adverbial adjunct of time acting as non-essential new interrupts a phased P when it is referring to the second group in phase:

Чле́нам па́ртии на́до ча́ще быва́ть в | The members of the party should attend
цеховы́х парторганиза́циях, в парт- | more frequently the workshop party
гру́ппах. | organisations, the party groups.
(Пра́вда, 13.11.66)

It may also on occasions interrupt a compound verbal group. Here the adjunct immediately preceding the compound P and the one interrupting it are stylistic variants. Compare the following two examples:

С тех пор моё представле́ние о нём | Since then my idea of him was always
всегда́ бы́ло свя́зано с э́тим прия́тным | connected with this pleasant dream.
сном.
(Paustovsky, Ска́зочник)

С их по́мощью в лаборато́риях | With their help in the world's labora-
ми́ра бы́ли впервы́е полу́чены мно́гие | tories there were obtained for the first
лека́рственные препара́ты. | time many medicinal preparations.
(Хи́мия и жизнь, 9.65)

When the adverbial adjunct of time acts as given, it is found at the beginning of the clause and separated from P by another clause element:

Тепе́рь он знал, что не́мец оди́н. | Now he knew that the German was
(Polevoy, По́весть о настоя́щем | alone.
челове́ке)

Обы́чно лю́ди стара́лись э́того не замеча́ть.

(Chakovsky, Неве́ста)

Usually people tried not to notice this.

One in six occurrences is found in this position.

This position and contextual role is especially typical of such adjuncts as тогда́, зате́м, неда́вно, сейча́с, тепе́рь:

Тогда́ Никола́й Константи́нович стал заде́рживаться на рабо́те, что́бы приходи́ть домо́й по́зже до́чери.

(Chakovsky, Неве́ста)

Then Nikolay Konstantinovich started to stay on at work in order to come home later than his daughter.

Неда́вно Комите́т наро́дного контро́ля СССР...вскрыл кру́пные недоста́тки в обслу́живании населе́ния.

(Изве́стия, 24.11.66)

Recently the People's Control Committee of the USSR...uncovered grave failings in [industries] serving the population.

When the adverbial adjunct of time acts as essential new, it is usually at the end of the clause:

[Но что переводи́ть на ру́сский язы́к?] Вопро́с возни́к не сего́дня.

(Литерату́рная газе́та, 28.6.67)

But what should be translated into Russian? This question didn't just arise today.

[Чья́-то неумоли́мая рука́ сбро́сила тебя́ вниз] и на́до начина́ть всё сно́ва.

(Granin, Иска́тели)

Someone's implacable hand has cast you down and you have to start everything again.

In this position the adverbial adjunct of time bears a greater emphasis by virtue of the fact that it occurs so rarely—only one occurrence in twenty is found in this position.

For even greater emphasis the adverbial adjunct of time is found with emphatic order of contextual elements either at the beginning of the clause or immediately preceding P. The essential new is realised by то́лько тогда́ and не всегда́ in the following examples:

То́лько тогда́ вы́ход кни́ги в Москве́ ста́нет по́длинным пра́здником для национа́льной литерату́ры.

(Литерату́рная газе́та, 28.6.67)

Only then will the publication of the book in Moscow become a real holiday for national literature.

Объедине́ние тече́ний в рабо́чем движе́нии не всегда́ мо́жет осуществля́ться на платфо́рме, отвеча́ющей коренны́м интере́сам пролетариа́та.

(Пра́вда, 4.11.66)

The union of the currents in the workers' movement cannot always be achieved on a platform corresponding to the basic interests of the proletariat.

(b) Preposition-plus-complement group

The adjunct of time realised by a preposition-plus-complement group (preposition-plus-complement adjunct of time) is most frequently found at the beginning of the clause acting as given:

В кану́н тру́дного и вели́кого двадца́-того ве́ка мне встре́тился ми́лый чуда́к и поэ́т Андерсен. (Paustovsky, Ска́зочник)	On the eve of the difficult and great twentieth century I met the dear eccentric and poet Andersen.
С 12 до 2x наступа́ет тишина́, ви́дно, лётчики обе́дают. (Изве́стия, 31.11.66)	From 12 till 2 a silence falls, evidently the pilots are having their dinner.

More than half of the occurrences are found in this position.

Next most frequently, the preposition-plus-complement adjunct of time is found at the end of the clause acting as essential new:

Случи́лось э́то в зи́мний ве́чер, всего́ за не́сколько часо́в до наступле́ния двадца́того столе́тия. (Paustovsky, Ска́зочник)	It happened on a winter's evening, just a few hours before the beginning of the twentieth century.
Мой «телохрани́тель» Тун, рове́сник моего́ Фе́ди, роди́лся в тот же год и ме́сяц — октя́брь 1942 го́да. (Изве́стия, 31.11.66)	My 'bodyguard' Tun, the same age as my Fedya, was born in the same year and month—October 1942.

A quarter of all occurrences are found in this position.

Acting as essential new, the preposition-plus-complement adjunct of time is occasionally found in the initial position, resulting in the emphatic order of contextual elements:

Уже́ в са́мом нача́ле войны́ ги́тлеров-ские войска́ стреми́лись прорва́ться че́рез Смоле́нск на Москву́. (Изве́стия, 5.12.66)	Right at the very start of the war Hitler's army tried to break through Smolensk to Moscow.

The preposition-plus-complement adjunct of time does not usually act as non-essential new. When it does so, it most frequently follows immediately after P:

В Сиракью́зском университе́те Крейн написа́л в 1891 г. ещё оди́н о́стрый памфле́т: «Иностра́нная поли́тика: три эпизо́да». (Изв АН СССР, сер лит и яз, vol. 24, 1965)	In Syracuse University Crane published in 1891 another sharply worded pam-phlet: *A Foreign Policy, in Three Glimpses.*

Only one occurrence in twenty is found in this position.

It may also immediately precede P. This usually happens when P is the final element in the clause and acts as essential new:

О́бщий объём выпуска́емой проду́к-ции с ка́ждым го́дом увели́чивается. (Литерату́рная газе́та, 28.6.67)	With every year the general volume of production grows.

To place the adjunct after P would leave it final in the clause, thus changing the contextual role.

When acting as non-essential new, the preposition-plus-complement adjunct of time may also interrupt a phased P when it refers to the first group in phase:

Морская волна́ не могла́ в тече́ние мно́гих лет смыть её [кра́ску] и́ли повреди́ть.

(Paustovsky, Ска́зочник)

The sea waves in the course of many years could not wash it [the paint] off or damage it.

(c) *Nominal group—accusative*

Adjuncts of time realised by a nominal group in the accusative case (accusative adjuncts of time), or in the genitive case if the adjunct is negative, are found equally frequently acting as given, essential or non-essential new.

When acting as given, the accusative adjunct of time is found at the beginning of the clause:

Почти́ де́сять лет он пла́вал на Ба́лтике, в Средизе́мном мо́ре.

(Изве́стия, 1.12.66)

For almost ten years he sailed in the Baltic, in the Mediterranean.

Мно́го лет спустя́ он со́здал великоле́пные стихи́ о свое́й тру́дной огненной мо́лодости.

(Литерату́рная газе́та, 14.6.67)

Many years later he wrote a magnificent poem about his difficult fiery youth.

When acting as essential new, it is found at the end of the clause:

Ты включа́ешь его́ де́сять, сто раз.

(Granin, Иска́тели)

You switch it on ten, a hundred times.

Туда́ забега́ешь ка́ждую свобо́дную мину́ту.

(Granin, Иска́тели)

You dash round there every spare minute.

When acting as non-essential new, two positions are possible— either immediately preceding or immediately following P. Negative adjuncts such as ни ра́зу, не раз, ни мину́ты always precede P:

Кудря́вцев ни ра́зу не спра́шивал, продолжа́ет ли Ва́ля встреча́ться с ним.

(Chakovsky, Неве́ста)

Kudryavtsev did not once ask whether Valya was continuing to meet him.

Accusative adjuncts of time whose head is realised by раз when acting as non-essential new precede P:

И. Абаши́дзе...и други́е ещё раз подчеркну́ли значе́ние э́того важне́йшего уча́стка де́ятельности тво́рческих сою́зов.

(Литерату́рная газе́та, 28.6.67)

I. Abashidze...and others once again underlined the significance of this most important section of the activity of the creative unions.

Otherwise, when acting as non-essential new, the accusative adjunct of time usually follows P:

Расска́з э́тот впервы́е был опублико́-
ван два го́да наза́д в «Литерату́рной
Росси́и».
(Литерату́рная газе́та, 14.6.67)

This story was published for the first
time two years ago in *Literary Russia*.

(d) Nominal group—genitive

Adjuncts of time realised by a nominal group in the genitive case
(genitive adjuncts of time) are usually found at the beginning of the
clause acting as given:

17 октября́ создаётся Кали́нинский
фронт.
(Изве́стия, 5.12.66)

On 17 October the Kalinin front was
set up.

Two-thirds of all occurrences are found in this position.

The genitive adjunct of time may occasionally be found immediately
following P acting as non-essential new:

Пе́рвый из них — «Не́сколько со-
ве́тов драмату́ргам» был опублико́-
ван 25 ноября́ 1893 г. в юмористи́-
ческом журна́ле «Йстина».
(Изв АН СССР, сер лит и яз,
vol. 24, 1965)

The first of them—*Some Hints for Play-
makers*—was published on 25 November
1893 in the humorous magazine *Truth*.

The genitive adjunct of time may also occasionally be found at the
end of the clause acting as essential new:

Расска́з «Смерть и дитя́» впервы́е
был опублико́ван 26 ма́рта 1898 г.
(Изв АН СССР, сер лит и яз,
vol. 24, 1965)

The story *Death and the Child* was first
published on 26 March 1898.

(e) Nominal group—instrumental

Adjuncts of time realised by a nominal group in the instrumental case
(instrumental adjuncts of time) most frequently precede P acting as
given:

Ещё днём по́зже [Кудря́вцев] сказа́л,
что ви́дел прокуро́ра.
(Chakovsky, Неве́ста)

Another day later [Kudryavtsev] said
that he had seen the judge.

На Покро́вку тёмными вечера́ми
сзыва́л нас Брик.
(Изв АН СССР, сер лит и яз,
vol. 24, 1965)

On dark evenings we were called together
to Pokrovka by Brik.

Almost half of all occurrences are found in this position.

When acting as non-essential new, the instrumental adjunct of time follows immediately after P:

Наприме́р, [Кудря́вцев] подойдёт ве́-
чером к окну́ и уви́дит, что Ва́ля
возвраща́ется домо́й не одна́.
(Chakovsky, Неве́ста)

For example, [Kudryavtsev] would go in the evening to the window and see that Valya was not returning home alone.

One in every seven occurrences is found in this position.

The adjunct поро́й (and поро́ю), however, usually immediately precedes P when acting as non-essential new:

Стихи́ с ри́фмами поро́ю пи́шутся
са́ми.
(Литерату́рная газе́та, 14.6.67)

Rhyming poems at times write themselves.

When it follows immediately after P, it is slightly more emphatic:

Аргуме́нтам э́тим вне́млют поро́й в
среде́ тво́рческой интеллиге́нции не
то́лько капиталисти́ческих, но и со-
циалисти́ческих стран.
(Литерату́рная газе́та, 29.10.66)

These arguments are listened to at times amongst the creative intelligentsia not only of the capitalist but also of the socialist countries.

When acting as essential new, instrumental adjuncts of time are found at the end of the clause:

Рабо́тают ноча́ми, пи́щу гото́вят при
све́те ламп, передвига́ются но́чью.
(Изве́стия, 31.11.66)

They work at nights, prepare food by the light of lamps, they move on at night.

Only one in every ten occurrences is found in this position.

(ii) Manner and degree

(a) Adverbial group

The adverbial adjuncts of manner and degree most frequently occur immediately preceding P acting as non-essential new:

По́зже э́то предположе́ние блестя́ще
подтверди́л его́ учени́к.
(Хи́мия и жизнь, 9.65)

Later this hypothesis was brilliantly confirmed by his pupil.

Обще́ственная жизнь ребя́т то́чно
воспроизводи́ла тогда́ обще́ственную
жизнь взро́слых.
(Chakovsky, Неве́ста)

The social life of the youngsters exactly copied at that time the social life of the grown-ups.

Almost seven out of every ten occurrences are found in this position.

This position is obligatory for all negative adverbial adjuncts of manner and degree—that is all those adjuncts immediately followed by the word не. This commonly occurs with the following words: во́все, отню́дь, почти́, совсе́м, as well as with words beginning with the morpheme ни-:

Разуме́ется, всё ска́занное вы́ше во́все не исче́рпывает пла́нов разви́тия нау́ки и те́хники в ближа́йшие го́ды. (Изве́стия, 11.11.66)	Of course everything which has been said above by no means exhausts the plans for the development of science and technology in the near future.
Я ника́к не мог поня́ть, почему́ нельзя́ ра́доваться ра́ньше како́го-нибудь твёрдого сро́ка. (Paustovsky, Ска́зочник)	I could not at all understand why one must not celebrate before some fixed time.

There are also a number of words which never act as essential new and which always immediately precede P. The commonest of these words are едва́, чуть, о́чень:

Лось едва́ успе́л сде́лать прыжо́к в кусты́. (Polevoy, По́весть о настоя́щем челове́ке)	The elk only just had time to jump into the bushes.
В ю́ности он о́чень люби́л ша́хматы [и постоя́нно уча́ствовал в студе́нческих турни́рах]. (Chakovsky, Неве́ста)	In his youth he had liked chess a lot and was always taking part in student tournaments.

The adverbial adjuncts of manner and degree are also found frequently preceding gerunds and participles:

Борьба́ за подъём се́льского хозя́йства ста́ла о́бщим де́лом тру́жеников го́рода и села́, ещё бо́лее скрепля́я их бра́тский сою́з. (Пра́вда, 31.12.66)	The struggle for the improvement of agriculture has become the common cause of the workers of the town and the country, forging even more tightly their brotherly union.
В большинстве́ и́збраны лю́ди с вы́сшим и́ли сре́дним образова́нием, хорошо́ зна́ющие произво́дство. (Пра́вда, 13.11.66)	On the whole men were chosen with higher or medium education, who knew the job well.

When the participle precedes the noun on which it depends, the adverbial adjuncts of manner and degree always precede P:

[Медве́дь] поню́хал его́ све́жие, вку́сно па́хнущие следы́. (Polevoy, По́весть о настоя́щем челове́ке)	[The bear] sniffed his fresh sweet-smelling tracks.

The adverbial adjuncts of manner and degree acting as non-essential new are also found immediately following P. This happens usually only when the adverbial group which realises the adjuncts of manner and degree is formed from a preposition-plus-complement group, now written as one word:

Пу́шкин...свинти́л воеди́но все сце́ны, кото́рые при ка́жущейся разобщённости и пестроте́ обрета́ют сквозно́е де́йствие.
(Изв АН СССР, сер лит и яз, vol. 24, 1965)

Pushkin...melded into a unit all the scenes which despite their apparent disparateness and variety acquire an unimpeded action.

If the adjuncts of manner and degree acting as non-essential new are in a clause together with a phased P, they will interrupt this P, provided that the adjunct refers exclusively to the second group in phase:

По́сле XXIII съе́зда коммуни́сты ста́ли реши́тельнее ста́вить вопро́с о пребыва́нии таки́х в ряда́х па́ртии.
(Пра́вда, 13.11.66)

After the 23rd congress the Communists began to ask with greater determination, whether such men should stay in the ranks of the party.

If the adjuncts of manner and degree acting as non-essential new are found in a clause with a compound P, they most frequently interrupt it:

«А́лый знак до́блести» был восто́рженно встре́чен англи́йской и затём и америка́нской кри́тикой 90-х годо́в.
(Изв АН СССР, сер лит и яз, vol. 24, 1965)

The Red Badge of Courage was received triumphantly by the English and later also by the American critics of the nineties.

They may also precede the whole of the compound P:

[Впервы́е э́то доказа́л...слон.] В его́ зуба́х случа́йно был обнару́жен фтор.
(Хи́мия и жизнь, 11.65)

It was the elephant...which first proved it. By chance fluorine was discovered in its teeth.

Next most frequently, the adverbial adjuncts of manner and degree act as essential new at the end of the clause:

Он был уве́рен, что узна́ет об э́том случа́йно.
(Chakovsky, Неве́ста)

He was sure that he would find out about it by chance.

Only one in every seven occurrences is found in this position.

For greater emphasis the adjunct may be modified by an emphatic word:

До а́вгустовской револю́ции 1963 го́да организа́ции, называ́вшие себя́ па́ртиями, не́ были похо́жи на них да́же отдалённо.
(Пра́вда, 7.12.66)

Before the August revolution of 1963 organisations calling themselves parties did not resemble them even remotely.

For even greater emphasis the adjunct is placed at the beginning of the clause. This results in the emphatic order of contextual elements (essential new preceding non-essential new):

Неда́ром О́дензе сла́вился свои́ми ре́зчиками по де́реву.
(Paustovsky, Ска́зочник)

It was not for nothing that Odense was famous for its wood carvers.

Мёдленно, óчень мёдленно Алексёй приоткрыл глазá.
(Polevoy, Пóвесть о настоя́щем человёке)

Slowly, very slowly Aleksey opened his eyes a little.

The force of this emphatic order of contextual elements is, however, somewhat weakened by rather frequent usage—one out of every six occurrences of the adjuncts of manner and degree acting as essential new is found with emphatic order of contextual elements.

Adverbial adjuncts of manner and degree do not usually act as given. The only word which is commonly found with this contextual function is так meaning 'in this way'. Acting as given, it is always found at the beginning of the clause, as in the second sentence of the following example:

Когда́ по кана́лу проходи́л корáбль, пу́шки стреля́ли холосты́ми заря́- дами…Так стáрый моря́к салютовáл свои́м счастли́вым товáрищам — ка- питáнам, ещё не ушёдшим на покóй.
(Paustovsky, Скáзочник)

When a ship passed along the canal, the cannons were fired with blank charges… In this way the old sailor saluted his fortunate colleagues—captains who had not yet gone to their rest.

(b) Preposition-plus-complement

The preposition-plus-complement adjuncts of manner and degree most frequently act as essential new at the end of the clause:

Писáтель стрóит свой мир по закóнам худóжественной вероя́тности.
(Изв АН СССР, сер лит и яз, vol. 24, 1965)

The writer constructs his world according to the laws of artistic probability.

Áндерсен вы́рос в бéдности.
(Paustovsky, Скáзочник)

Andersen grew up in poverty.

Half of all the occurrences are found in this position.

The preposition-plus-complement adjuncts of manner and degree are also occasionally found acting as essential new at the beginning of the clause with the emphatic order of contextual elements:

И́менно на э́том при́нципе стрóится егó рассказ.
(Изв АН СССР, сер лит и яз, vol. 24, 1965)

It is on just this principle that his story is constructed.

Next most frequently, the preposition-plus-complement adjuncts of manner and degree act as non-essential new. One occurrence in five is found with this contextual role. Two positions are possible—either immediately preceding or immediately following P. The following types of adjunct are found preceding P. First, adjuncts of degree:

Своéй полúтикой раскóла рабóчего движéния прáвые социáл-демокрáты в огрóмной стéпени облегчúли прихóд фашúзма к влáсти в Гермáнии.
(Прáвда, 4.11.66)

By its policy of splitting the workers' movement the right-wing Social Democrats to a large extent facilitated the coming to power of Fascism in Germany.

Secondly, adverbial expressions of manner. There are a number of groups which, though formed from a preposition plus complement, behave as if they were adverbial groups. These very often have the preposition с with such nouns as вкýсом, гóрдостью, рáдостью, сúлой, трудóм, удовóльствием, успéхом, чéстью. This is illustrated in the second sentence of the following example:

Нéкоторое врéмя спустя́ Кудря́вцева вы́звали в обкóм пáртии и предложúли рабóту в совнархóзе. Он с рáдостью согласúлся.
(Chakovsky, Невéста)

Some time later Kudryavtsev was called to the district committee of the party and offered work on the Local Council. He gladly accepted.

These adverbial expressions are also found with other prepositions:

Он в спéшке постáвил стáрую батарéю.
(Granin, Искáтели)

He had hurriedly put in the old battery.

Note that these expressions are often translated into English by an adverb.

Otherwise, the adjunct of manner, acting as non-essential new, immediately follows P:

Онó [эпúческое врéмя] присýтствует как бы в «сжáтом» вúде в жúвописи.
(Изв АН СССР, сер лит и яз, vol. 24, 1965)

It [epic time] is present as if in a 'compressed' form in painting.

The adjuncts which precede P acting as non-essential new will interrupt a phased P when referring to the second group in phase:

Мóжно без преувеличéния сказáть, что подавля́ющее числó больши́х откры́тий...бы́ло бы невозмóжно сдéлать без пóмощи микроанáлиза.
(Хúмия и жизнь, 10.66)

One can say without exaggeration that the vast majority of great discoveries... could not have been made without the help of microanalysis.

They may also interrupt a compound P:

Достúгнутые úми сущéственные завоевáния за послéдний перúод бы́ли в огрóмной стéпени обуслóвлены еди́нством дéйствий коммунúстов и социалúстов.
(Прáвда, 4.11.66)

The important gains which they have achieved in the last period were to a large extent a result of the unity of the actions of the Communists and the Socialists.

The preposition-plus-complement adjuncts of manner and degree may also act as given at the beginning of the clause. This is the least usual contextual role but is found more frequently for preposition-plus-complement groups than for adverbial groups. Almost a quarter of all the occurrences of preposition-plus-complement adjuncts of manner and degree are found in this position. It is illustrated in the following example:

С нýдным ожесточéнием он допы́тывается, почемý этот кóнтур помещён спрáва а не слéва.
(Granin, Искáтели)

With a tedious persistence he questions why this contour is placed on the right and not on the left.

(iii) Place

(a) Adverbial group

The adverbial adjunct of place is most frequently found at the end of the clause acting as essential new. Almost one out of every three occurrences is found in this position. This is most common with adverbial adjuncts expressing direction:

Ты прогоня́ешь всех домóй.
(Granin, Искáтели)

You chase everyone home.

Рабóчее движéние ускóренным шáгом идёт вперёд.
(Прáвда, 4.11.66)

At an increased pace the workers' movement is going forward.

Almost six out of every ten occurrences of adjuncts expressing direction are found in this position.

Adverbial adjuncts expressing position are less frequently found at the end of the clause:

Нéмец потоптáлся вóзле.
(Polevoy, Пóвесть о настоя́щем
человéке)

The German stamped around nearby.

Only one out of every seven occurrences of adjuncts expressing position is found at the end of the clause.

Very occasionally, the adverbial adjunct of place is found at the beginning of the clause acting as essential new with the emphatic order of contextual elements:

Мóжет быть, и́менно здесь они́ сказáлись прéжде всегó и отчётливее всегó.
(Литератýрная газéта, 6.10.66)

Perhaps, it was just here that they had their earliest and most distinctive effect.

The adverbial adjunct of place is found next most frequently at the beginning of the clause acting as given. One in every four occurrences is found in this position. In contrast to those at the end of the clause, the

69

adjunct expressing position is most frequent at the beginning of the clause:

Вокру́г черне́ли го́ры, лес.
(Изве́стия, 1.12.66)

Around were silhouetted the mountains, the forests.

Здесь обнару́живаются две взаимоисключа́ющие кра́йности.
(Литерату́рная газе́та, 29.10.66)

Here one discovers two mutually exclusive extremes.

One in every three occurrences of these adjuncts is found in this position.

The adjunct expressing direction is much more rarely found in this position:

Сюда́ зимо́й и ле́том прихо́дят охо́тники, молодёжь с заво́да.
(Изве́стия, 1.12.66)

Here in winter and summer come hunters, young men from the factory.

Only one in every ten occurrences of these adjuncts is found in this position.

The adverbial adjunct of place may also act as non-essential new. This is usually an adjunct expressing direction. These are found immediately following P:

Че́рез не́сколько дней Ва́ля сно́ва пришла́ домо́й по́здно.
(Chakovsky, Неве́ста)

A few days later Valya again came home late.

В сле́дующем году́ он привози́т сюда́ во вновь осно́ванное зимо́вье свою́ ю́ную жену́.   (Изве́стия, 1.12.66)

In the following year he brings here to his newly established winter quarters his young wife.

One in every four occurrences of these adjuncts is found in this position.

Otherwise, only negative adjuncts are usually found immediately preceding P:

...чтобы помога́ть ма́тери — немолодо́й боле́зненной же́нщине, кото́рая никогда́ нигде́ не рабо́тала.
(Chakovsky, Неве́ста)

...to help his mother, an old ailing woman, who had never worked anywhere.

(b) Preposition-plus-complement group

The preposition-plus-complement adjunct of place is most frequently found at the end of the clause acting as essential new. Almost one in every two occurrences is found in this position. This is especially common with adjuncts expressing direction, as in the second and third clauses in the following example:

Когда́ оте́ц сказа́л Ва́ле об э́том, она́ пошла́ в свою́ ко́мнату, се́ла на крова́ть и запла́кала.
(Chakovsky, Неве́ста)

When her father told Valya about it, she went to her room, sat on her bed and started to cry.

Almost seven out of every ten occurrences are found in this position.

Adjuncts of position are also found frequently at the end of the clause acting as essential new:

Я не хочу́ бо́льше ви́деть э́того
человѐка у нас в до́ме.
(Chakovsky, Неве́ста)

I do not want to see this man any more in our house.

Almost four out of every ten occurrences are found in this position.

When acting as essential new, adjuncts of place may also be found at the beginning of the clause with the emphatic order of contextual elements (essential new before non-essential):

И́менно в расска́зах я нахожу́ наи-
бо́льшее тво́рческое удовлетворе́ние.
(Литерату́рная газе́та, 14.6.67)

It is precisely in the stories that I find the greatest creative satisfaction.

The preposition-plus-complement adjunct of place is next most frequently found at the beginning of the clause acting as given. About a quarter of all occurrences are found in this position. This is more common with adjuncts expressing position:

В гора́х на берегу́ бу́рной реки́ по-
стро́ен ма́ленький одноэта́жный
оте́ль. (Изве́стия, 1.12.66)

In the mountains on the bank of a stormy river a small one-storeyed hotel had been built.

More than three out of every ten occurrences are found in this position. These adjuncts are not necessarily found right at the beginning of the clause, they sometimes follow another adjunct—usually one of time:

21 апре́ля 1894 г. в том же журна́ле
был опублико́ван друго́й сатири́чес-
кий расска́з Кре́йна — «Ночь в клу́бе
миллионе́ров».
(Изв АН СССР, сер лит и яз,
vol. 24, 1965)

On 21 April 1894 in the same magazine there was published another satirical story by Crane—*A Night at the Millionaire's Club.*

An adjunct of time always precedes one of place when both are acting as given at the beginning of the clause.

Adjuncts expressing direction are comparatively rarely found at the beginning of the clause acting as given:

Из По́то-По́то в Бако́нго в центр
тяну́лись це́лые челове́ческие пото́ки.
(Пра́вда, 7.12.66)

From Poto-Poto in Bacongo to the centre there stretched whole streams of people.

Only one occurrence in ten is found in this position.

The preposition-plus-complement adjunct of place is comparatively rarely found acting as non-essential new. When doing so, it usually follows immediately after P. Only one occurrence in ten is found in this position. It is equally infrequent for adjuncts expressing position and direction:

Юного поэ́та встре́тил среди́ цвето́ч- | The young poet met amidst the flower
ных клумб рой краси́вых де́вушек — | beds a swarm of beautiful girls—grand-
вну́чек ста́рого капита́на. | daughters of the old captain.
(Paustovsky, Ска́зочник)

Не́сколько лет спустя́ А́ндерсен попа́л | Several years later Andersen came to this
в э́ту уса́дьбу уже́ студе́нтом. | estate when already a student.
(Paustovsky, Ска́зочник)

Occasionally, when acting as non-essential new, the preposition-plus-complement adjunct of place may come immediately before P. In this position it bears more emphasis:

Нове́лла на трёх-четырёх страни́цах | The story in three or four pages depicted
запечатле́ла челове́ческую жизнь в её | human life in its natural flow.
есте́ственном тече́нии.
(Изв АН СССР, сер лит и яз,
vol. 24, 1965)

When acting as non-essential new the preposition-plus-complement adjunct of place may interrupt a phased P, if it refers to the first group in phase only:

Я не собира́юсь в да́нной статье́ | I am not going in the present article to
рассма́тривать те сло́жные перипети́и, | examine the complex peripetia which
кото́рые пережива́ет вчера́шняя мо- | recent young prose writers are ex-
лода́я про́за на пути́ к зре́лости. | periencing on the path to maturity.
(Литерату́рная газе́та, 22.11.66)

(iv) Cause, aim and condition

Adjuncts of cause, aim and condition behave identically. They are all usually realised by a preposition-plus-complement group. They are found equally frequently at the beginning and at the end of the clause. Adjuncts found in both of these positions account for eight occurrences out of every ten. When at the end of the clause, they act as essential new:

Ка́ждый из них по-но́вому прочтёт и | Each one of them will read again both
Пу́шкина и Шо́лохова, откро́ет в них | Pushkin and Sholokhov, will discover
мно́гое, что ра́ньше бы́ло недосту́пно | in them much that was inaccessible
из-за плохо́го зна́ния языка́. | before because of a poor knowledge of
(Литерату́рная газе́та, 28.6.67) | the language.

На́ша наро́дная интеллиге́нция...не | Our people's intelligentsia...will not
жале́ет сил для выполне́ния зада́ний | spare any efforts to fulfil the tasks of the
пятиле́тки. | five year plan.
(Пра́вда, 31.12.66)

Но они́ соглаша́ются предоста́вить | But they agree to let the latter [the right-
после́дним [пра́вым социали́стам] э́ту | wing socialists] take over this role on
роль то́лько при одно́м усло́вии — | only one condition—a complete with-
по́лном отка́зе социали́стов от кла́ссо- | drawal of the Socialists from their class
вых пролета́рских пози́ций. | proletarian point of view.
(Пра́вда, 4.11.66)

Occasionally, the adjuncts of cause, aim and condition are found at the beginning of the clause acting as essential new with the emphatic order of contextual elements:

Именно из-за Воло́ди он наста́л ра́ньше.
(Chakovsky, Неве́ста)

It was just because of Volodya that it had come earlier.

At the beginning of the clause the adjuncts of cause, aim and condition much more frequently act as given:

От ожида́ния внеза́пно вспы́хивающих фонаре́й у меня́ замира́ло се́рдце.
(Paustovsky, Ска́зочник)

From the expectation that the lamps would suddenly flash on, my heart stopped beating.

Для проведе́ния опера́ции «Тайфу́н» ги́тлеровское кома́ндование сосредото́чило на моско́вском направле́нии огро́мные си́лы.
(Изве́стия, 5.12.66)

To carry out operation 'Typhoon' the Hitler command concentrated on the Moscow front huge forces.

Они́...изуча́ют вое́нное де́ло, чтобы в слу́чае необходи́мости с ору́жием в рука́х защити́ть револю́цию.
(Пра́вда, 7.12.66)

They...study military matters so that they can, if it proves necessary, defend the revolution with a weapon in their hands.

Occasionally, adjuncts of cause, aim and condition are found immediately following P acting as non-essential new:

Алексе́й нажа́л для прове́рки гаше́тки...
(Polevoy, По́весть о настоя́щем челове́ке)

To check Aleksey pressed the triggers...

(v) Concession

The adjunct of concession is usually realised by a preposition-plus-complement group. It almost always acts as given and is found either at the beginning of the clause:

Несмотря́ на всё э́то, «Молода́я гва́рдия» сыгра́ла тем не ме́нее свою́ значи́тельную роль в собира́нии молоды́х сил литерату́ры.
(Изв АН СССР, сер лит и яз, vol. 24, 1965)

Despite all this, *The Young Guard* nevertheless played a significant part in the gathering of the young forces of literature.

or preceding P:

Молоды́е [писа́тели] второ́й полови́ны пятидеся́тых годо́в, при всей свое́й я́ркой тала́нтливости, уступа́ли свои́м непосре́дственным предше́ственникам в гла́вном: в глубине́ и зре́лости пережива́ния жи́зни.
(Литерату́рная газе́та, 22.11.66)

The young [writers] of the second half of the fifties, with all their brilliant talent, were inferior to their direct predecessors in what was most important: in the depth and maturity of their experience of life.

The adjunct of concession may occasionally act as essential new. It is usually found with the emphatic order of contextual elements. The essential new in the following example is indicated by italics in the original:

Наш Пу́шкин *вопреки́ жела́ниям власте́й* подня́лся на верши́ну духо́вной жи́зни своего́ вре́мени.
(Литерату́рная газе́та, 27.9.66)

Our Pushkin *despite the wishes of the authorities* ascended to the summit of the spiritual life of his time.

(*vi*) *Agency*

(*a*) *Preposition-plus-complement*

Most frequently the preposition-plus-complement adjunct of agency acts as essential new in the final position:

Пи́щу гото́вят при све́те ламп.
(Изве́стия, 31.11.66)

Food is prepared by the light of the lamps.

Almost half of all occurrences are found in this position.

Next most frequently, the preposition-plus-complement adjunct of agency is found preceding P acting as given. It may be at the beginning of the clause:

Че́рез де́йствия просты́х солда́т и описа́ние их тяжёлых бу́дней Крейн развенчивает «геро́ику» войны́.
(Изв АН СССР, сер лит и яз, vol. 24, 1965)

Through the actions of the simple soldiers and a description of their difficult everyday life Crane deprives the 'heroism' of war of its glory.

but it need not necessarily be so:

На берегу́ при све́те фа́келов то́же идёт рабо́та.   (Изве́стия, 31.11.66)

On the shore by the light of torches work is also going on.

Almost a third of all occurrences are found preceding P.

Occasionally, the preposition-plus-complement adjunct of agency is found immediately following P acting as non-essential new:

[Он] хо́чет идти́ на я́хте по следа́м откры́тий Бошняка́.
(Изве́стия, 1.12.66)

[He] wants to follow by yacht in the tracks of Boshnyak's discoveries.

(*b*) *Nominal group—instrumental*

Most frequently, the instrumental adjunct of agency is final in the clause acting as essential new:

Тогда́ ма́льчик замени́л по́длинные спекта́кли вообража́емыми.
(Paustovsky, Ска́зочник)

Then the boy replaced real shows with imaginary ones.

Over half the occurrences are found in this position.

Next most frequently, the instrumental adjunct of agency acts as non-essential new immediately following P:

Óбо всём э́том мо́жно писа́ть рас-ска́зы и ска́зки — таки́е ска́зки, что лю́ди бу́дут то́лько кача́ть голова́ми от удивле́ния.

(Paustovsky, Ска́зочник)

One could write stories and fairy tales about all this—such tales that people would just shake their heads in surprise.

Almost one in every five occurrences is found in this position.

The instrumental adjunct of agency is also found at the beginning of the clause acting as given:

Э́тим Фо́ллетт не то́лько изврати́л смысл всего́ сбо́рника но и лиши́л его́ его́ обличи́тельной стороны́.

(Изв АН СССР, сер лит и яз, vol. 24, 1965)

By this means Follett not only distorted the meaning of the whole collection, but also deprived it of its accusatory force.

3. ORDER OF WORDS IN THE NOMINAL GROUP

The most important factor determining the order of words in the nominal group is grammatical. The position of the nominal group modifier in relation to the head varies according to the class of modifier but each class of modifier has a definite position in the nominal group which is fixed by grammatical rules. With some classes of modifier these grammatical rules may be relaxed and variations in position become possible. Here one notes contextual and stylistic factors influencing the order of words. Each class of nominal group modifier will now be examined separately.

A. *Adjectives*

The adjectival modifier in Russian usually precedes the noun on which it depends. It may follow for reasons which may be contextual, stylistic or grammatical.

(i) *Contextual*

In a nominal group standing at the end of a clause the adjectival modifier may follow the nominal head when it is acting as essential new and the nominal head as non-essential new. Very frequently the noun does not indicate a specific object but is a general word, merely classifying the area of applicability of the adjective. The nominal head in these structures is often realised by a noun such as челове́к, де́ло, вещь. So important is the adjectival modifier that the clause often becomes meaningless if it is omitted. The omission of the word нешу́точное in the following example renders the sentence nonsensical:

Разгу́лин понима́л: получи́ть две́сти пятьдеся́т пудо́в зерна́ с гекта́ра — де́ло нешу́точное.

(Babayevsky, Кавале́р золото́й звезды́)

Razgulin realised: to get two hundred and fifty puds of grain per hectare is no laughing matter.

Alternatively, the noun may have already occurred in the text and, as a result, in the sentence in which the noun is repeated the main emphasis falls on the adjective. The noun in itself is meaningful but in context it is almost completely meaningless, so much so that the omission of the adjective renders the sentence nonsensical. Thus the adjective вы́год-ным could not be omitted from the last sentence of the following example:

Я попроси́л но́вую знако́мую отвести́ меня́ по́сле база́ра в Тально́во и подыска́ть избу́, где бы стать мне квартира́нтом. Я каза́лся квартира́н-том вы́годным.

(Solzhenitsyn, Матрёнин двор)

I asked my new friend to take me after the market to Tal'novo and find a hut where I could become a lodger. It seemed that I was a profitable lodger.

It is not essential for the noun to be repeated in the text. If the noun has little meaning to communicate in a particular context, so that the main emphasis falls on the adjective, it may follow the noun. A little later in the Solzhenitsyn story from which the last example came the following sentence is found:

Здесь не нашло́сь ко́мнаты отде́ль-ной, бы́ло те́сно и шу́мно.

(Solzhenitsyn, Матрёнин двор)

Here there wasn't a separate room, it was crowded and noisy.

Once again the omission of the adjective (in this case отде́льной) would make nonsense of the sentence. The author is not telling one that there wasn't a room, but that there wasn't a *separate* room. The following clause confirms this.

Occasionally, not only does the adjectival modifier follow the nominal head, but it is separated from the head by one or more clause elements:

Урожа́и получа́ем больши́е.

(Изве́стия, 31.11.66)

The harvests we get are big.

Ме́сто ты указа́л действи́тельно гри-бно́е.

(Неде́ля, 27.11.69)

The place you pointed out is really full of mushrooms.

In both these examples the nominal head acts as given, P as non-essential new and the adjectival modifier as essential new.

It must be pointed out that there is no hard and fast rule stating that an adjectival modifier *must* follow the nominal head when it acts as essential new and the nominal head as non-essential new. All one notes is a tendency, especially strong where the noun is a general word. In other words, although there are contextual reasons to justify the order of adjectival modifier following nominal head, it is only a stylistic alternative of the more usual order of adjectival modifier preceding the nominal head. One can see in this a conflict between the contextual tendency to place the most important element final in the clause (as is illustrated in the above examples) and the grammatical rule which places adjectival modifiers before nominal heads. The following examples show that sometimes the grammatical rule prevails:

Двáдцать лет — хорóшая вещь.
(Simonov, Дни и нóчи)

Twenty years is a fine thing.

Слáва э́тих людéй — э́то пóдлинная слáва.
(Fadeyev, Молодáя гвáрдия)

The glory of these men is real glory.

Despite valid contextual reasons, the adjectival modifier precedes the noun. There is no difference in emphasis between these sentences and the preceding ones.

(ii) Stylistic

Apart from this type of stylistic variation, there are two others. First, an adjectival modifier may follow the nominal head, though both are acting as given:

Ветрáми студёными выдувáло из неё [избы́] печнóе грéво не срáзу.
(Solzhenitsyn, Матрёнин двор)

The freezing winds did not blow the warmth from the stove out of it [the hut] all at once.

ветрáми студёными is a less usual stylistic variant of студёными ветрáми.

Secondly, if the adjectival modifier has dependent on it a submodifier realised by a rank-shifted preposition-plus-complement or nominal group, the adjectival modifier may precede or follow the head. The submodifier always follows the modifier. In the following example the adjectival modifier нóвую has dependent on it a rank-shifted preposition-plus-complement group submodifier по свои́м организациóнным и полити́ческим при́нципам; both follow the head пáртию (H—M—MM). The head acts as non-essential new, the modifier and submodifier as essential new:

полити́ческий дéятель, создáвший пáртию пролетариáта, совершéнно нóвую по свои́м организациóнным и полити́ческим при́нципам.
(Недéля, 3.11.69)

a politician, who created a party of the proletariat, completely new in its organisational and political principles.

In the following example the adjectival modifier ненýжному and the

rank-shifted nominal group submodifier людям both precede the head
щенку (M—MM—H):

по отношению к беспомощному не-
нужному людям щенку...
    (Kazakov, Арктур — гончий пёс)

in relation to the helpless puppy not
needed by man...

The following two factors influence the order:

(*a*) the complexity of the submodifier. The simpler the structure of
the submodifier, the likelier it is to precede the head; the more complex
the structure of the submodifier, the likelier it is to follow the head. The
more complex structure M—MM following H is also more likely to act
as essential new;

(*b*) the type of text. The more formal the text, the likelier it is for a
complex submodifier to precede the head; the more popular the text,
the likelier it is for a complex submodifier to follow the head.

(*iii*) *Grammatical*

If the head of a nominal group is an indefinite pronoun such as чтó-то,
нéчто, кóе-что, ктó-то, the adjectival modifier always follows the
pronominal head:

Он сказáл чтó-то непонятное, злóе.
    (Kazakov, На полустáнке)

He said something incomprehensible,
evil.

Я хотéл взять кóе-что посущéст-
веннее.
    (Недéля, 27.11.69)

I wanted to take something a little more
essential.

Adjectival modifiers also follow negative pronouns:

В нём нé было ничегó злóго.
    (Solzhenitsyn, Матрёнин двор)

There was nothing evil in him.

The adjective also follows in proper names such as Пётр Велúкий
(Peter the Great), Ивáн Грóзный (Ivan the Terrible).

Before leaving the subject of adjectival modifiers, one further problem
must be discussed—the order of two adjectival modifiers both preceding
the head. The order depends on the exact relationship between the two
modifiers and the head. Two relationships are frequently found:

(i) The first adjectival modifier modifies the second one and the
head as a unit: M—(M—H). Here the order is fixed. The second
modifier and head in this type includes at one extreme adjective plus
noun in set phrases such as товáрный пóезд (a goods train), зубнóй
врач (a dentist). Any adjective modifying such a set phrase will precede

both parts of it: дли́нный това́рный по́езд (a long goods train), ста́рый зубно́й врач (an old dentist).

This type of relationship is also commonly found other than in set phrases. For example:

Да здра́вствует геро́йческое колхо́зное крестья́нство. (Неде́ля, 20.10.69)	Long live the heroic collective farm peasantry.

This is an opening sentence of an article on the collective farm peasantry and, therefore, геро́йческое refers то колхо́зное крестья́нство as a whole. Had the article been concerned with the heroic peasantry, the order of the adjectival modifiers would have been reversed, because in this case the author would have been discussing the heroic peasantry who came from collective farms and not, as here, the collective farm peasantry who are heroic.

(ii) The two adjectival modifiers both equally modify the head; they list qualities about one object: M—M—H:

Была́ па́смурная холо́дная о́сень. (Kazakov, На полуста́нке)	It was an overcast cold autumn.
дрему́чие, непрохо́жие леса́ (Solzhenitsyn, Матрёнин двор)	primeval, impenetrable forests
Необходи́мо просто́е и му́жественное де́ло. (Неде́ля, 20.10.69)	We need a simple and courageous deed.

Here, the subject of discussion is not cold autumn which is overcast, or impenetrable forests which are primeval, or a courageous deed which is simple, but autumn which is both cold and overcast, forests which are both primeval and impenetrable and a deed which is both simple and courageous. The order of the modifiers is interchangeable. Sometimes, however, complex lexical rules determine that the adjectival modifiers occur in a particular order:

большо́й, чёрный во́рон (Gorky, Злоде́и)	a big black raven

Here the adjective of size precedes that of colour and no other order is likely.

Punctuation frequently, though by no means always, helps by inserting a comma between the two adjectives as in the second and fourth examples but not in the first one. The possibility of the presence of the linking word и, as in the third example, also distinguishes this type.

One sometimes finds a combination of both types in which the first modifier modifies the following two as well as the head, while the second and third equally modify the head: M—(M—M—H):

мировáя коммунистѝческая и рабóчая пáртия (Неде́ля, 20.10.69)	the world Communist and Workers' party

Thus the order of the adjectival modifiers of the first type depends on their grammatical relationship, while that of the second type usually depends on stylistic considerations.

в. *Deictics*

(*i*) *Possessives*

Possessive deictic modifiers most frequently precede the head. They can, however, also follow. In this case they are almost meaningless, and in this respect resemble the personal pronoun subject following the predicator instead of its more usual position preceding it (see p. 31). Compare the force of the two occurrences of её in the following paragraph:

Меня́ порази́ла её речь. Она́ не говори́ла, а напева́ла уми́льно и слова́ её бы́ли те са́мые, за кото́рыми потяну́ла меня́ тоска́ из Áзии. (Solzhenitsyn, Матрёнин двор)	I was struck by her speech. She did not talk but intoned with feeling and her words were just those for which homesickness had drawn me from Asia.

The first occurrence precedes its noun because it is meaningful—it tells one whose speech struck the author, while the second occurrence has little if any meaning: it is obvious from the context whose words are being referred to. The possessive modifier may also be found between an adjectival modifier and the head. Here, too, it has little meaning:

просто́рная изба́ и осо́бенно прио-ко́нная её часть... (Solzhenitsyn, Матрёнин двор)	the spacious hut and especially the part by the window...

(*ii*) *Demonstratives*

Demonstrative deictic modifiers also usually precede the head and any adjectival modifier present:

в те благослове́нные времена́ (Неде́ля, 20.10.69)	in those blessed times

така́я жесто́кая эконо́мия (Неде́ля, 27.10.69)	such a cruel economy

э́та ненасы́тная ло́гика (Неде́ля, 27.10.69)	this insatiable logic

When following the head, like the possessive deictic modifiers, the demonstrative modifiers are almost meaningless:

У бе́рега стоя́ла при́стань, па́хнувшая рого́жей, кана́том, сыро́й гни́лью и во́блой. На при́стани э́той ре́дко кто сходи́л.
(Kazakov, Аркту́р — го́нчий пёс)

On the bank stood a jetty, which smelled of bast, rope, damp decay and roach. Hardly anyone got off at this jetty.

The demonstrative modifier тако́й, when it has dependent on it a submodifier realised by как and a nominal or preposition-plus-complement group, may precede or follow the head. The two positions are stylistic variants:

тако́й неторопли́вый индиви́д как я...
(Неде́ля, 27.10.69)

such an unhurried individual as I...

прия́тные ли́ца — таки́е как у на́ших това́рищей...
(Неде́ля, 20.10.69)

pleasant faces—such as our comrades have...

The submodifier usually follows the noun whether the modifier precedes or follows. It may, on very rare occasions, precede the noun:

и́менно о таки́х как он лю́дях говори́ли: беспарти́йный большеви́к...
(Неде́ля, 24.11.69)

it was precisely about such men as he that people said: non-party Bolshevik...

(iii) Quantitatives and serials

Both these types of deictics precede the head and any adjectival modifier present:

обраще́ние ко всем революцио́нным комите́там
(Неде́ля, 20.10.69)

an appeal to all the revolutionary committees

вдохнове́ние мно́гих замеча́тельных актёров
(Неде́ля, 20.10.69)

the inspiration of many remarkable actors

Ка́ждой го́нчей соба́ке необходи́мо одобре́ние.
(Kazakov, Аркту́р — го́нчий пёс)

Every hunting dog needs encouragement.

от други́х субтропи́ческих дере́вьев
(Gladkov, По́весть о де́тстве)

from other subtropical trees

When a quantitative deictic modifier occurs in the same nominal group as another deictic, the quantitative deictic precedes any other, whether the latter is possessive:

всем свои́м существо́м...
(Неде́ля, 20.10.69)

with all his being...

demonstrative:

все э́ти попы́тки...   all these attempts...
    (Неде́ля, 27.10.69)

or serial:

интере́сы любо́го друго́го госуда́р-   the interests of any other state
ства
    (Неде́ля, 27.10.69)

c. *Numerals*

A numeral modifier precedes the head unless an approximate number is
being stated, in which case it follows the head. Compare:

Рабо́та рассчи́тана на три дня...   The work is calculated to last three
    (Неде́ля, 27.10.69)   days...

with:

побро́див часа́ два...   having wandered around for about two
    (Неде́ля, 20.10.69)   hours...

The numeral, when preceding the head, usually precedes the adjectival
modifier as well:

...я́вится ещё одно́й ва́жной ве́хой... ...will be one more important land-
    (Неде́ля, 20.10.69)   mark...

However, if a quantitative deictic and a numeral modifier both precede
the head, the quantitative deictic precedes both the numeral and the
head and refers to the numeral and the head as a unit—i.e. Deictic—
(Num—H):

все шестна́дцать киломе́тров   all sixteen kilometres
    (Неде́ля, 20.10.69)

це́лых два́дцать мину́т   a whole twenty minutes
    (Неде́ля, 27.10.69)

Similarly, such words as после́дний, сле́дующий, and ordinal numerals
also precede the numeral modifier:

после́дние де́сять мину́т   the last ten minutes

d. *Rank-shifted nominal group*

The rank-shifted nominal group modifier almost always follows the
head, whether it is in the genitive:

смысл повседне́вного существо-   the sense of everyday existence...
ва́ния...
    (Solzhenitsyn, Матрёнин двор)

82

dative:

по́мощь това́рищу в бою́... (Kozhevnikov, Семь дней)	help for a comrade in battle...

or instrumental case:

руково́дство людьми́ (Chakovsky, Неве́ста)	leadership of men

However, if the head of the nominal group modifier is realised by the word ро́да, it usually precedes the head:

Она́ далеко́ не сра́зу ста́ла выбира́ть тако́го ро́да пе́сни. (Литерату́рная Росси́я, No. 10, 1969)	It was not right at the start that she began to choose for herself songs of such a kind.

When following an adjectival modifier, the genitive nominal group modifier may also precede the head, when both modifiers are listing two equipollent qualities of the head—i.e. M—M—H. It is most frequently found in the description of a person's appearance:

ху́денькая, невысо́кого ро́ста же́н-щина (Pavlenko, Сча́стье)	a thin short woman

If, however, the genitive nominal group modifier refers to both the adjectival modifier and the nominal head as a unit, it will resume its more usual position following the head—i.e. (M—H)—M:

бри́тый подборо́док квадра́тной фо́р-мы (Kuprin, Листриго́ны)	a clean-shaven chin of a square shape

E. *Rank-shifted preposition-plus-complement group*

The rank-shifted preposition-plus-complement modifier almost always follows the head:

мечта́ о ти́хом уголке́ Росси́и (Solzhenitsyn, Матрёнин двор)	a dream about a quiet corner of Russia

When following an adjectival modifier, it may also precede the head, if it lists two equipollent qualities about one head—i.e. M—M—H:

широ́кий из то́лстой же́сти я́щик (Serafimovich, Стре́лочник)	a broad thick tin box

If, however, the preposition-plus-complement modifier refers to both adjectival modifier and head, it follows the head—i.e. (M—H)—M:

рябо́й па́рень в ко́жаном пальто́ (Kazakov, На полуста́нке)	a pock-marked boy in a leather coat

(cf. the identical structure with the genitive nominal group modifier above).

Rank-shifted clause modifier

Rank-shifted clause modifiers usually follow the head:

Пра́во называ́ться её сы́ном ли́бо до́черью де́лает челове́ка чле́ном вели́кой и дру́жной семьи́. (Неде́ля, 3.11.69)	The right to be called its son or daughter makes a man a member of a great and harmonious family.

Thus, in the above example, the rank-shifted clause modifier называ́ться её сы́ном ли́бо до́черью follows the head пра́во. This order is obligatory for all rank-shifted clause modifiers except those bound by a participle. These may precede:

постановле́ние то́лько что со́зданного сове́тского прави́тельства... (Неде́ля, 20.10.69)	an edict of the newly created Soviet government...

or follow the head:

пе́рвые декре́ты, при́нятые II съе́здом сове́тов... (Неде́ля, 20.10.69)	the first decrees issued by the second Congress of Soviets...

If the structure of the rank-shifted clause modifier consists only of a participle *preceded* by an adjunct, it will always precede the head. This is commonly an adjunct of place, time (as in the second example in this subsection) or a negative adjunct:

никогда́ не произнесённое и́мя... (Kazakov, Аркту́р — го́нчий пёс)	a name which had never been uttered...

Otherwise, only tendencies, not firm rules, can be indicated. If the rank-shifted clause modifier is short, consisting of only two unmodified elements—the predicator and either a complement or an adjunct—it tends to precede the head:

о я́кобы име́ющей ме́сто «национа́льной вражде́» (Неде́ля, 20.10.69)	concerning the 'national enmity' which apparently existed
посма́тривая на пронося́щиеся ми́мо автомаши́ны (Kazakov, Аркту́р — го́нчий пёс)	taking a look at the cars going past

Rank-shifted clause modifiers with a more complex structure usually follow the head:

честь, ока́занную мне в связи́ с мои́м 60-ле́тием (Пра́вда, 20.12.66)	the honour extended to me in connection with my 60th birthday

Sometimes the rank-shifted clause modifier follows for contextual reasons. In a nominal group at the end of a clause the head may be a general word acting as non-essential new, while the modifier acts as essential new:

Всё э́то не про́сто «долитерату́рная биогра́фия» писа́теля, а жизнь, про-жи́тая с геро́ями бу́дущих книг.
(Изв АН СССР, сер лит и яз, vol. 24, 1965)

All this is not simply the 'pre-literary biography' of the writer but a life lived with the heroes of future books.

G. *Adverbs*

The adverbial modifier follows the head. In the following example there are two adverbs—of time and place:

возвраще́ние ра́ньше сро́ка домо́й
(Неде́ля, 27.10.69)

his return home before time

H. *Parenthetic words*

Parenthetic modifiers referring to one nominal group, and not to the clause as a whole, usually precede the nominal group head and any adjectival modifier present:

Прибы́в в заполя́рный го́род в ка́честве, допу́стим, фина́нсового ре-визо́ра...
(Неде́ля, 27.10.69)

Having arrived in the polar town, as, let us assume, a finance inspector...

BIBLIOGRAPHY

'Word order'

Adamec, P. *Порядок слов в современном русском языке.* Prague, 1966.

Borras, F. M. & Christian, R. F. *Russian Syntax* (pp. 376–88). Oxford University Press, 1959.

Chistyakova, A. L. 'Взаимопорядок подлежащего и сказуемого в повествовательном предложении', *Русский язык в школе.* Просвещение, Moscow, 1954, No. 6, 5–10.

Galkina-Fedoruk, E. M. (ed.). *Современный русский язык, ч. 2: морфология, синтаксис* (pp. 449–57). МГУ, Moscow, 1964.

Gorbachik, A. L. 'Об изучении порядка слов в русском языке', *Из опыта преподавания русского языка иностранцам.* МГУ, Moscow, 1964, 158–76.

Gvozdyov, A. N. *Современный русский литературный язык, ч. 2* (3rd ed.) (pp. 16–18, 164–74). Просвещение, Moscow, 1968.

Larokhina, N. M. 'Функции порядка слов в русском языке и методика работы над порядком слов', *Методика преподавания русского языка иностранцам.* МГУ, Moscow, 1967, 129–42.

Listvinov, N. G. *Вопросы стилистики русского языка, ч. 2* (pp. 106–54). Высшая партийная школа, Moscow, 1962.

Rogova, K. A. 'Место прямого дополнения в простом повествовательном предложении', *Ученые записки ленинградского государственного университета, серия филологических наук.* No. 302, 1962, 40–50.

'Об изучении порядка слов в простом предложении', *Русский язык для иностранцев.* Учпедгиз, Moscow, 1963/4, 93–106.

Rozental', D. E. *Практическая стилистика русского языка* (2nd ed.) (pp. 226–41). Высшая школа, Moscow, 1968.

Schaller, H. M. *Die Wortstellung im Russischen.* Sagner, Munich, 1966.

Sirotinina, O. B. *Порядок слов в русском языке.* Saratov, 1965.

Unbegaun, B. O. *Russian Grammar* (pp. 296–304). Oxford University Press, 1957.

Vinogradov, V. V. (ed.). *Грамматика русского языка* (2nd ed.) (vol. 2, part 1, pp. 658–91). АН СССР, Moscow, 1960.

Grammatical analysis

Halliday, M. A. K. 'Categories of the theory of grammar', *Word.* New York, 1961, III, 241–92.

'Linguistics and its application to teaching', *Patterns of language: Papers in general, descriptive and applied linguistics.* Longmans, London, 1966, 1–41.

Halliday, M. A. K., McIntosh, A., Strevens, P. D. *The linguistic sciences and language teaching.* Longmans, London, 1964.

Ward, D. *The Russian Language Today.* Hutchinson, London, 1965.

Contextual analysis

Garvin, P. L. 'Czechoslovakia', *Current trends in linguistics—Soviet and East European linguistics.* Mouton, The Hague, 1963, 502–8.

Kovtunova, I. I. 'Принципы словорасположения в современном русском языке', *Русский язык. Грамматические исследования.* Наука, Moscow, 1967, 96–146.

Krushel'nitskaya, K. G. 'К вопросу о смысловом членении предложения', *Вопросы языкознания,* Moscow, 1956, No. 5, 55–67.

Mathesius, V. *Čeština a obecný jazykopyt.* Prague, 1947.

Raspopov, I. P. *Актуальное членение предложения.* Ufa, 1961.

For EU product safety concerns, contact us at Calle de José Abascal, 56–1°, 28003 Madrid, Spain or eugpsr@cambridge.org.